*I S...*

# I Step, I Mount

## The Vision of
## John Henry Newman

*Compiled by*
*Robert Van de Weyer and Pat Saunders*

LAMP

Marshall Morgan and Scott
Lamp Press
34–42 Cleveland Street, London, W1P 5FB U.K.

First published in 1989 by Marshall Morgan and Scott Publications
Ltd. Part of the Marshall Pickering Holdings Group

British Library Cataloguing in Publication Data

Newman, John Henry, *1801–1890*
   I step, I mount.
   1. Christian life
   I. Title   II. Van de Weyer, Robert, *1950–*
   III. Saunders, Pat
   248.4

   ISBN 0-551-01915-8

Text Set in Baskerville by Prima Graphics, Camberley, Surrey
Printed in Great Britain by Cox & Wyman Ltd., Reading

I step, I mount where He has led;–
   Men count my haltings o'er;–
I know them; yet, though self I dread,
   I love His precept more.

                    'Sensitiveness'

Other titles in *The Vision of . . .* series include:

*Lament and Love: George Herbert*
*The Spiritual Kiss: St. Aelred*
*Measureless to Man: Samuel Taylor Coleridge*

# Contents

# Introduction

John Henry Newman, in common with St Paul, is not easy to like; yet if one persists, he is profoundly inspiring, and ultimately quite lovable. At first encounter he seems arrogant and self-assertive, certain of the rightness of whatever views he is currently holding, and witheringly dismissive of those with whom he disagrees. He is obsessed with his own spiritual journey, writing voluminously about every twist and turn of his soul, and is insistent that his friends and associates defer to his spiritual authority. He shows little outward warmth and affection, and in his sermons and books any natural passion is firmly encased within strict logical argument.

Yet he was a true servant of God. Even as a young man people recognised that, despite his impressive intellect and prodigious output, he was wholly lacking in personal ambition; he sincerely wanted to put his abilities at God's disposal, even if it meant a life of dull obscurity. At various times in his life he devoted himself to the pastoral care of the poor, first in a village in Oxfordshire, and later in Birmingham; and he never doubted that this work was more important in God's eyes than all his writing and lecturing. And he was endearingly shy, awkward and taciturn in large groups, but vivacious and witty amongst his close friends to whom he was always loyal and generous.

Newman shares a further characteristic with St Paul: one cannot get away from him. Just as almost every doctrinal debate eventually comes back to Paul's theology, so almost every major issue that has faced the Church in our day was foreshadowed in the writings of

Newman. As a young man Newman, with Keble and Pusey, led the Oxford Movement whose influence has now permeated the whole Church, bringing the sacraments back into the centre of Christian worship. In an age when science seemed to be disproving many of the central tenets of the Christian faith, Newman taught that religion had nothing to fear from free scientific enquiry, since the basic truths seen through the eye of faith would ultimately be affirmed by science – and only false doctrines would be disproved. In a somewhat perverse way Newman was a pioneer of the ecumenical movement: in the first half of his life as an Anglican he strove to reawaken the Church of England to its Catholic heritage, especially the teaching of the early fathers; and in the second half of his life as a Roman Catholic he sought to open the Catholic Church to more liberal influences, and to give Catholics greater freedom from the central power of Rome. He risked the charge of heresy for asserting the importance of the laity as the ultimate guardians of the faith, and urging the Pope and the bishops to consult the laity on matters of doctrine and morality. And, as a puritan in his personal tastes and way of life, he taught that worship could be solemn and reverent, and yet simple and unfussy, without elaborate ritual and costly ornament. It has often been remarked that Newman's spirit presided over the Second Vatican Council, which in the past quarter century has brought revolutionary change in the Catholic Church.

Yet throughout all his teaching over almost seventy years, dealing with a wide range of different subjects, there is a single theme that consistently re-emerges: that Christian doctrine is nothing unless it is put into practice in people's lives. He had no time for academic theology or doctrinal debate which did not have as its ultimate purpose the conversion of souls and the enrichment of human life. He believed that personal holiness should be the fruit of true doctrine, and that the insights given by theology should deepen our love and inspire our worship of God. He himself thought nothing of outward success and status; and when in 1872 he was thrown out of St Paul's by a verger for his scruffy appearance, he was mightily amused. Yet by the end of his life, Protestants and Catholics alike had come to admire the depth, the courage, and, above all, the sincerity of his faith; he became, despite himself, the grand old man of Victorian Christianity.

*     *     *

Newman was born in 1801, the eldest son of a London banker. He was sent to a boarding school in Ealing where at the age of fifteen, under the influence of an evangelical master, Walter Mayers, he experienced a conversion. In 1817 he went up to Trinity College, Oxford, where he worked hard and impressed his tutors; but during the final examinations he broke down, and his poor result was a profound blow to his self-confidence. But despite this he sat for a fellowship at Oriel College, and was elected in 1822. In the liberal atmosphere of the common room this shy, reclusive young man gradually made friends and learnt to enjoy intellectual debate, and his evangelical theology broadened to embrace a much wider range of Christian thought – in particular the teachings of the early fathers of the Church. In 1824 he was ordained in the Church of England, and four years later became vicar of St Mary's Church in Oxford. His sermons, in which he taught that the early fathers should provide the basis for the doctrines of the Church of England, attracted growing attention, especially amongst the university undergraduates.

In 1832 he went on a tour of the Mediterranean where he had his first close contact with the Roman Catholic Church. He was repelled by what he saw as the Catholic idolatory of the Virgin Mary and the saints, yet he was also impressed by the beauty of many of the churches, and by a sense that, amidst the apparent heresies, here was a tradition unbroken since the first apostles. Most of his poetry was written in this period, and after a serious illness in Sicily on his way home he wrote his most famous poem, *Lead, kindly Light.* He now believed he had a mission to heal the wounds within the Church of England caused by the Reformation, and to rediscover her roots within the early Church.

Others within Oxford already shared this vision, and in 1833 he joined with two other young men, John Keble and Edward Pusey, in what came to be known as the Oxford Movement. They preached sermons and published tracts on every aspect of church life, comparing the present practices of the Church of England unfavourably with those prescribed by the early fathers. They sought to restore the sacraments to a central place in church worship, and advocated that the Church should be independent and free of political influence. At first, the movement enjoyed astonishing success, but gradually opposition grew. In 1841 Newman was condemned by many bishops and by the university for the publication of Tract 90 in which he argued that the Thirty-nine Articles of the Church of England were political rather than doctrinal in character, and should be re-interpreted in the light of Catholic tradition.

Newman, although he had invited controversy, was shocked at the anger and abuse directed at him, and, in 1842, he withdrew to Littlemore, a village near Oxford, where he could think and pray in peace. He adopted a monastic discipline, and for three years he lived as a recluse. Gradually he realised that his views, if pressed to their conclusion, were incompatible with member-ship of the Anglican Church; and he came to believe that the Roman Catholic Church, for all its faults, was the only true inheritor of the ancient faith. So he resigned from St Mary's, and on 9 October 1845 he was received into the Catholic Church.

Newman now went to college in Rome where, like a young undergraduate, he attended lectures in Catholic theology. Returning to England, he established an Oratory in Birmingham, a community of priests following a simple rule of life, and this became his home for the rest of his days. In 1852 he went to Ireland as rector of the new Catholic university there; and although he disliked the job itself – and missed his community in Birmingham – it caused him to reflect deeply on the nature of education. He wrote a remarkable book on the purpose and nature of a university, in which he asserted that a firm religious basis to education was compatible with free scientific enquiry – a notion highly suspect amongst the Catholic hierarchy at the time. Back in England in 1859 he took over the editorship of the *Rambler*, a Catholic journal hitherto run by lay people. Within a few months he was forced to resign after writing an article advocating that the laity should be consulted on religious matters: Newman claimed that the laity understood the content of the faith instinctively, through the power of the Holy Spirit, and that in past centuries it had been the laity rather than the Pope and bishops who had saved the Church from heresy. So shocking was such an idea that Newman came under suspicion in Rome as a heretic; and although he was not denounced, his reputation was now at its lowest ebb.

The tide turned, however, in 1864 when Charles Kingsley wrote an article accusing Newman of hypocrisy and dishonesty. After Newman had written an open letter defending himself, Kingsley published a long pamphlet accusing Newman of secretly seeking to undermine the Church of England. This led Newman to write an entire book, the *Apologia Pro Vita Sua*, telling the story of his own spiritual and theological development. The book was widely read, and Newman's sincerity was proved beyond doubt to both Catholic and Anglican readers alike. Within the country as a whole Newman's reputation suddenly rose, and even old Anglican friends who had avoided him for twenty years renewed their friendship. Newman now believed his mission on earth was complete, and in the expectation of imminent death he wrote *The Dream of Gerontius*, a poetic drama of a soul being received into the after-life. But in fact he lived for a further quarter of a century, preaching and writing with greater authority and influence than ever before.

During this latter period of his life, he played a typically perverse role in the early stages of the ecumenical movement in Britain. Catholic ideas and practices had continued to spread within the Church of England, and some of Newman's former associates, such as Pusey, began to hope for union between the Anglican and Roman Churches. The Roman Catholic Church for its part was becoming more extreme in its attitudes. Newman sought to dampen the hopes of Pusey and his fellow Anglicans, since, having been both an Anglican and a Catholic, Newman realised that the obstacles to unity were far greater than such optimists imagined. But equally he resisted the extremist tendencies in the Roman Catholic Church. In particular he was strongly against any attempt to define the Pope's infallibility, believing this would be a severe blow to long-term hopes of unity between Catholics, Protestants and Orthodox; and when the First Vatican Council did declare the Pope to be infallible, Newman argued that this only applied in very restricted circumstances where he was expressing the beliefs already held by the Church.

Despite a lifetime in the thick of controversy, Newman was finally accepted and revered by those who had once vilified him. In 1877 he was elected the first honorary fellow of Trinity College, Oxford, where he had been an undergraduate more than half a century earlier. And in 1879 he was made a cardinal by Pope Leo XIII. But, although now famous throughout England and across Europe, Newman in his final years spent an increasing amount of time within the Oratory school he had founded in Birmingham. He preached to the school each Sunday, giving religious instruction to the senior boys, and helped produce an annual Latin play.

He died on 11 August 1890. Two days later his old friend, R W Church, then Dean of St Paul's, started his obituary in *The Guardian* with these words: 'Cardinal Newman is dead, and we lose in him not only one of the greatest masters of English style, not only a man of singular purity and beauty of character, not only an eminent example of personal sanctity, but the founder, we may almost say, of the Church of England as we see it.'

\*　　\*　　\*

Most people today have heard of Cardinal Newman, but very few read his works. His most famous work, *The Apologia*, seems turgid and laborious to the modern reader; and his sermons and theological works, elegant though they are in style, no longer stir us because we have long since accepted the ideas for which Newman had to fight so passionately. Even his great hymn, *Lead, kindly Light*, is now rarely sung because it lacks a setting which is attractive to the modern ear.

Yet amidst his voluminous writing there are passages which speak with remarkable warmth and wisdom to our time; and it is these which we have tried to select for this volume. We make no attempt to give a rounded picture of his ideas, but rather enable Newman to speak across the gulf which separates the nineteenth century from the present age. He was an untiring correspondent, and over 20,000 of his letters have been preserved; these, along with the private journals he kept at various times in his life, give a profound insight into his spiritual journey. Thus the first part of this book is extracts from his letters and journals, following the course of his long life. The second part concerns his ideas, and consists of pieces taken from a wide range of his published works; they are ordered according to the subject they cover rather than the works from which they come. The final part is selections from his poetry: although he was not a great poet, some of his poems are small masterpieces, while others are poignant expressions of his own innermost feelings.

If this volume helps to resurrect Newman's works from the graveyard of unread classics, to be appreciated by a new generation who can learn much from his penetrating intellect and courageous spirit, it will have served a valuable purpose.

# LIFE

# Early Years

*Extract from Newman's journal reflecting upon his conversion at the age of fifteen, an experience which convinced him that he was 'elected to eternal glory'.*

1. On my conversion. How the wisdom and goodness of God is discerned – I was going from school half a year sooner than I did – my staying arose from 8th of March (1816). Thereby I was left at school by myself, my friends gone away – that is, it was a time of reflection, and when the influences of Mr Mayers would have room to act upon me. Also, I was terrified at the heavy hand of God which came down upon me.

2. The reality of conversion: as cutting at the root of doubt, providing a chain between God and the soul (i.e. with every link complete). I know I am right. How do you know it? I know I know. How? I know I know I know &c &c.

Again, every action tells, has weight and meaning. No shadows – consistency. The unconverted man changes his end with his time of life, or goes on changing about – but here it is all reality.

\*

*Letter to his brother Francis describing his feelings prior to his final examinations at Oxford.*

August 17, 1820

Here at Oxford I am most comfortable. The quiet and stillness of every thing around me tends to calm and lull those emotions, which the near prospect of my grand examination and a heart too solicitous about fame and too fearful of failure are continually striving to excite. I read very much certainly, but I may say (I trust), without deceiving myself or losing sight of my unnumbered transgressions, that God sanctifies my studies by breathing into me all the while thoughts of Him, and enables me to praise Him with joyful lips, when I rise and when I lie down, and when I wake in the night. I know not how in words to describe my state. If I look at the mercies of God, my soul is bright; when I view myself from a different point of view, I wonder how I can dare to assert any growth in grace. I am in dread now, lest I should have written anything presumptuous. For the calm happiness I now enjoy I cannot feel thankful as I ought. How in my future life, if I do live, shall I look back with a sad smile at these days! however, I am weak, dark, and cold now, and then I trust I shall be strong in the faith, light and fervent.

As to the event of the examination, 'it is in the Lord's hands; let Him do, as it seemeth to Him good'. It is my daily, and (I hope) heartfelt prayer, that I may not get any honours here, if they are to be the least cause of sin to me. As the time approaches, and I have laboured more at my books, the trial is greater. May God give me strength still to say, 'Let me get no honours, if they are to be the slightest cause of sin to me.' And do you, my dear Francis, pray for me in the same way.

*

*Letter to his father in the wake of his failure in the final examinations.*

December 1, 1820

It is all over, and I have not succeeded. The pain it gives me to be obliged to inform you and my mother of it, I cannot express. What I feel on my own account is indeed nothing at all, compared with the thought that I have disappointed you. And most willingly would I consent to a hundred times the sadness that now overshadows me, if so doing would save my mother and you from feeling vexation. I will not attempt to describe what I have gone through, but it is past away, and I feel quite lightened of a load. The examining masters were as kind as it was possible to

12

be; but my nerves quite forsook me and I failed. I have done everything I could to attain my object; I have spared no labour, and my reputation in my college is as solid as before, if not so splendid. If a man falls in battle after a display of bravery, he is honoured as a hero; ought not the same glory to attend him who falls in the field of literary conflict?

*

*Extracts from his journal analysing his character and behaviour, and in particular his attitudes towards his younger brothers, Charles and Francis.*

August 4, 1821

I have this week been preparing myself for the Sacrament, which, God willing, I hope to take with my brother Francis once a fortnight during the Long Vacation. These are my answers to Doddridge's Questions in His Rise and Progress.

Praised be God, I think I am much more resigned to Him than I was, more contented, less careful of the morrow, less desirous of the things of the world.

I am very deficient in spirituality in prayer, in brotherly love, meekness, humility, forgiveness of injuries, charity, benevolence, purity, truth, and patience.

I am very bad-tempered, vain, proud, arrogant, prone to anger, and vehement.

But I principally wish to attain a strength of faith, of which at present I feel the want very much. Every now and then momentary clouds of doubt cross my mind ... but though thus afflicted, I have, what may God in his mercy continue, a 'full assurance of hope', concerning my final perseverance, and have had it from the time of my conversion. I am also in great want of a fervent love towards Christ.

September 1, 1821

I have this fortnight been secured from temptation more than former weeks; I have not had so many opportunities of being proud, contentious, and ill tempered.

About last Tuesday week, on the recollection and self reproach of hastiness and heat in conversation, I requested Francis always to look at me, as a hint against the danger.

I have also behaved, I trust, more kindly to Charles than before.

But I have sinned against truth not seldom; and have been constantly impatient at Francis.

I trust I have prayed more frequently . . . and have felt the peace and love of God diffused on my heart. I have interceded more frequently for others.

So cold a veil does not seem to separate me from my Father. I am not so distant from Charles, and he, thank God, expressed himself pleased yesterday, when reading with us, with Scott's Commentary.

O God, grant me to grow in grace daily, and continually to examine myself, that I may always know how my accounts stand, whenever called upon to reckon for my stewardship.

## Life in Oxford

*Extracts from a letter to his brother Charles, concerning his election to a fellowship at Oriel College, Oxford.*

April 13, 1822

Now that the contest and labour is all over, I may be allowed to state, that for the last month or two I have been so far from having a mean opinion of myself, which my Mother some how judged I had conceived, that I have actually considered myself as having a very good chance of succeeding, at the approaching examination. Instead of saying in the letter I wrote about six weeks ago, '*I* think I have no chance', I merely stated the opinion of every one else.

I am then fellow of Oriel; and, though unable at present to define the advantages that follow, I know enough to say with confidence and thankfulness that I have gained independence, competency, and literary society. Not that I expect any immediate emolument, but I have gained a spell which can conjure me as many pupils as I can desire.

The examination throughout was most kind and considerate, and we were supplied with sandwiches, fruit, cake, jellies, and wine – a blazing fire, and plenty of time.

I think myself honoured inexpressibly by being among such kind, liberal, candid, moderate, learned and pious men, as every act shows the fellows of Oriel as a body to be. There's a eulogium for you!

Yesterday I took my seat in Chapel, and dined with a large party in the Common Room. Today I have breakfasted and dined there, and shall in future, as a constant thing. I sat next to Keble yesterday at dinner, and, as I have heard him represented, he is more like an undergraduate than the first man in Oxford – so perfectly unassuming and unaffected in his manner.

Thus, not by the might of my arm, but by circumstances as seemingly unaccountable in themselves as those by which I lost my class, I am fellow of Oriel. I hope I have not been vain in anything I have said. I am tied up at Oxford by my pupil, or I should like much to run up. I have not yet gone to the Bank about the money, for which thank my Father.

Keep this letter as I may wish to refer to it. Now indeed

'I groan no more
Chained to the literary oar.'

\*

*Extracts from his journal written around the time of his ordination in the Church of England on Trinity Sunday 1824.*

As the time approaches for my ordination, thank God, I feel more and more happy. Make me Thy instrument ... make use of me, when Thou wilt, and dash me to pieces when Thou wilt. Let me, living or dying, in fortune and misfortune, in joy and sadness, in health and sickness, in honour and dishonour, be Thine.

Sunday, June 13

It is over. I am thine, O Lord; I seem quite dizzy, and cannot altogether believe and understand it. At first, after the hands were laid on me, my heart shuddered within me; the words 'for ever' are so terrible. It was hardly a godly feeling which made me feel melancholy at the idea of giving up all for God. At times indeed my heart burnt within me, particularly during the singing of the Veni Creator. Yet, Lord, I ask not for comfort in comparison of sanctification ... I feel as a man thrown suddenly into deep water.

Sunday, August 15

Two Sermons a week are very exhausting. This is only the third week, and I am already running dry .... The question of regeneration perplexes me very much.

*

*Extract from a letter to his father replying to his father's concern that he was over-enthusiastic in visiting his parishioners.*

August 9, 1824

So far from this invasion of 'an Englishman's castle' being galling to the feelings of the poor, I am convinced by facts that it is very acceptable. In all places I have been received with civility, in most with cheerfulness and a kind of glad surprise, and in many with quite a cordiality and warmth of feeling. One person says, 'Aye, I was sure that one time or other we should have a proper minister – ' another that 'she had understood from such a one that a nice young gentleman was come to the parish –' a third 'begged I would do him the favour to call on him, whenever it was convenient to me' (this general invitation has been by no means uncommon). Another, speaking of the parish she came from said, 'the old man preached very good doctrine but he did not come to visit people at their houses as the new one did.' Singularly enough, I had written down as a memorandum a day or two before I received your letter, 'I am more convinced than ever of the necessity of frequently visiting the poorer classes – they seem so gratified at it, and praise it.' Nor do I visit the poor only – I mean to go all through the parish; and have already visited the shopkeepers and principal people. They, it is obvious, have facilities for educating their children, which the poor have not – and on that ground it is that a clergyman is more concerned with the children of the latter; though our church certainly intended that not only schoolmasters of the poorer children, but all schoolmasters, high and low, should be under her jurisdiction. The plan was not completed, and we must make the best of what we have got.

I have not tried to bring over any regular dissenter – indeed I have told them all, 'I shall make no difference between you and churchgoers – I count you all my flock, and shall be most happy to do you a service out of Church, if I cannot within it.' A good dissenter is of course incomparably better than a bad Churchman – but a good Churchman I think better than a good dissenter. There is too much irreligion in the place for me to be so mad as to drive away so active an ally as Mr Hinton seems to be.

Thank you for your letter, and pardon my freedom of reply.

*

*Extract from his journal, written in April 1828, soon after the death of his sister, Mary.*

And now how can I summon strength to recount the particulars of the heaviest affliction with which the good hand of God has ever visited me ... Here every thing reminds me of her. She was with us at Oxford, and I took a delight in showing her the place – and every building, every tree, seems to speak of her. I cannot realise that I shall never see her again.

It is thirteen weeks tomorrow since we lost her. She was taken ill at dinner this day thirteen weeks, January 4. Spasms came on in the night, the next morning she was dying – she died at 20 minutes past 9 p.m. on Saturday, the 5th.

Hawkins was elected Provost January 31, went up to Town February 1, and celebrated the great day of the College on the 2nd. Keble stood a good chance of being Provost.

I am just entering upon St Mary's as Vicar; thus am I taken from literary work to Parochial.

Pusey is to be married after Easter – he has been very ill, and some months at Brighton for his health.

Keble published his *Christian Year* last summer. Dear Mary learned many of them by heart. They were a comfort to her in her acute pain. Mr Mayers has died suddenly.

For some time I had a presentiment more or less strong that we should lose dear Mary. I was led to this by her extreme loveliness of character, and by the circumstance of my great affection for her. I thought I loved her too well, and hardly ever dared to take my full swing of enjoyment in her dear society. It must have been in October 1826 that, as I looked at her, beautiful as she was, I seemed to say to myself, not so much 'will you live?' as 'how strange that you are still alive!'

I have much to try me in the way of money matters.

A's debts are not far short of £500 (I think in the event £700). Frank and I paid this sum between us.

## Mediterranean Travels

*Extract from a letter to his mother, upon visiting Malta.*

January 22, 1833

I have seen St John's Church, and most magnificent it is. It is in the same style as St Peter's; in richness and exactness, minuteness and completeness of decoration, far exceeding anything I have ever seen. I shall go to it once or twice more to get some more accurate notion of it. It is built with a nave with side aisles leading to separate chapels or altars, e.g. the French chapel, the Italian, the Spanish. It is covered throughout with the most costly marbles and with gilding; a multitude of pictures – some very fine – some statuary, splendid tapestries, and silver lamps and candlesticks of course. In the Chapel of the Communion are the famous silver rails which were saved from the clutches of Bonaparte by being painted to look like wood; he took away the gold rails. By this and similar acts the French have made themselves hated here. The Knights of St John (the Baptist, not the Evangelist) were not allowed to leave away their property, accordingly immense sums were available for religious works. It is said they brought from Rhodes property to the amount of 300,000*l.* a year.

I have hitherto seen little of the Greek and Latin churches, but what I have seen fires me 'with great admiration'. I do not perceive that my opinion has in any respect changed about them; but it is fearful to have before one's eyes the perversion of all the best, the holiest, the most exalted feelings of human nature. Everything in St John's Church is admirable, if it did not go too far; it is a beautiful flower run to seed. I am impressed with a sad presentiment, as if the gift of truth when once lost was lost for ever. And so the Christian world is gradually becoming barren and effete, as land which has been worked out and has become sand. We have lasted longer than the South, but we too are going, as it would seem.

As to the number of sects which have split off from the Church, many of them have already ended in Socinianism and heresy worse than any in Rome or Constantinople. All this does not interfere with good men being in any Church, nor is there any proof that we have more than they, though if you cut away from us those who are in no sense Churchmen, though called so, I think there are more in us, as far as appearances go. By-the-bye, what answer do Protestants make to the *fact* of the Greek Church invoking saints, over-honouring the Virgin, and substituting ceremonies for a 'reasonable service', which they say are the prophetic marks of Anti-Christ? I do not see that the Romanists are more than advanced Greeks, the errors being the same, though less in degree in the latter.

*

*Extract from a letter to his mother, upon visiting Rome.*

April 5, 1833

As to the *Roman* Catholic system, I have ever detested it so much that I cannot detest it more by seeing it; but to the Catholic system I am more attached than ever, and quite love the little monks (seminarists) of Rome; they look so innocent and bright, poor boys! and we have fallen in, more or less, with a number of interesting Irish and English priests. I regret that we could form no intimate acquaintance with them. I fear there are very grave and far-spreading scandals among the Italian priesthood, and there is mummery in abundance; yet there is a deep substratum of true Christianity; and I think they may be as near truth at the least as that Mr B., whom I like less and less every day.

*

*Extracts from a letter to his friend, John Christie, who became a supporter of the Oxford Movement, giving an account of his vist to Rome.*

April 6, 1833

Till I got here, I have had little leisure to write to any of my friends. I shall regret Rome very much; it is a delightful place, so calm and quiet, so dignified and beautiful, that I know nothing like it but Oxford; and, as being the place of martyrdom and burial of some of the most favoured instruments of God, it has an interest and a solemn charm which no other place can possess except Jerusalem. Before the remains of the Saints the grandeur of pagan Rome crumbles as utterly as have its material structures, and in the ruins which lie scattered on all sides we do but see the 'disjecta membra' of the fourth monster of Daniel's Vision. I confess, I cannot enter into, rather I protest against, the state of mind of those who affect a classical enthusiasm at the sight of Rome.

As to my view of the Romanist system, it remains, I believe, unchanged. A union with Rome, while it is what it is, is impossible; it is a dream. As to the individual members of the cruel church, who can but love and feel for them? I am sure I have seen persons in Rome, who thus move me, though they cast out our name as evil. There is so much amiableness and gentleness, so much Oxonianism (so to say) such an amusing and interesting demureness, and such simplicity of look and speech, that I feel for those indeed who are bound with an iron chain, which cripples their energies, and (one would think) makes their devotion languid. What a strange situation it is, to be with those who think one in a stage of perdition, who speak calmly with one, while they have awful thoughts!

21

what a mixture of grief and indignation, what a perplexity between frankness and reserve comes over one!

Next Tuesday, we go our separate ways; the Froudes homeward, I drawn by an irresistible attraction to the fair levels and richly verdured heights of Sicily. What a country it is! a shadow of Eden, so as at once to enrapture and to make one melancholy. It will be a vision for my whole life; and, though I should not choose, I am not sorry to go alone, in order, as Wordsworth would say, to commune with high nature. I hope to be home at all events not later than the beginning of June. I want to set-to again at my book. I trust I shall be conducted back safely, to be made use of. I do not mind saying this, for I do not think I am actuated by ambitious views, though power, when possessed or in prospect, is a snare. At present to me it is neither in possession or prospect; so let me enjoy my freedom from temptation, while I am sheltered from it; and, should it be ordained that I am never to have the temptation, so much the happier for me. At present I can truly say that I would take the lot of retirement, were the choice offered to me, provided I saw others maintaining instead of me those views which seem to me of supreme and exclusive importance. But I am talking great nonsense, and cannot think how I have come to say it, though I do not know why I should be ashamed of it either, for in matter of fact we of Oxford have a high place in trying times of the Church.

*

*Letter to his pupil, Henry Wilberforce, recounting his illness in Sicily; it was during this illness that he wrote his famous poem 'Lead kindly Light'.*

July 16, 1833

I have been so tired and languid since my return, that I have written no letter which I was not driven to write – else you were in my thoughts – and I hoped you would hear of my return some how or other. I was tired from my journey, having been up 6 nights out of the last 7; – which shows my strength. Indeed I must not call it strength, meaning by that any inherent thing, for my strength is as if the mercy of God externally holds me up day by day. All sorts of evils came upon me in Sicily – the fever, of which many were dying on all sides of me, and which in some places was so bad that they in their fright called it cholera, was but one though the greatest (*perhaps*) of the (before strange to me) complaints which suddenly fell upon me (in connection with it). For a week and more my nurses, etc., thought I could not recover – no medicine was given me which could grapple with the disorder – they know nothing of calomel – they bled me indeed, but took away so little blood that both Mr Babington and Dr Ogle say, it could be of no use to me – in fact the fever ran its course; and when the crisis came, I was spared – and immediately after gained strength in a surprising way. I was so reduced, I could not lift my hand to my mouth to feed myself – much less rise, or (again) sit up, in bed – in four or five days' time I could (with help) walk about the room – and in ten days I was able to travel to Palermo – performing one day a journey of 60 miles over a rough country. A determination of blood to my head came on, as I was getting well – but it has gradually gone off, as I get strength. (August 4.–) The only remaining signs of my indisposition now are my hair falling off, and a slight cough, which is very slight. I was taken ill first in Catania, after spending two nights (unwilling) in the open air, which I believe is a very dangerous thing in Sicily. However it could not be called more than weakness, and I was able to proceed on my journey. When I got to Leonforte in the very heart of the country, I broke down. For three days I lay without any medical assistance – on the morning of the fourth a notion seized me that my illness was all fancy, so I set out on my mule. After proceeding about 7 miles in great distress from a sort of suffocating feeling, I was forced to betake myself to a hut by the wayside, where I lay the greater part of the day. On a sudden I found fingers at my pulse – a medical man happened by chance to be in a neighbouring cottage and they called him in. His prescription enabled me to get on that evening to Castro Giovanni, the ancient Enna, where I was laid up for 3 weeks. Thence I travelled to Palermo; where the time I had to wait for a vessel was of material service to me in the way of recruiting. After another delay of 3 weeks I set out for Marseilles, and it being the season of calms, was a whole fortnight on the water. Thence I came to England with all speed; and not till I got home, could persuade myself I was not in a dream. So strange has every thing been to me.

I hope it was not presumptuous, but from the beginning of my illness I had so strong a feeling on my mind that I should recover, that, whatever I did in the way of preparation for death (I mean, of giving my servant directions about letters, etc.) was done as a mere matter of duty. I could not help saying, 'I must act as if I were to die, but I think God has work for me yet.' – Thus I cannot answer your questions, never having realised eternity as about to break upon me. Yet I had many serious thoughts. It was a lonely situation I found myself in, at Leonforte, at a miserable inn. I am not sure my mind was quite clear at all times, so as to be sensible of its desolateness – yet I had once, doubtless when I felt myself lonely, quite a revelation come upon me of God's love to His elect, and felt as if I were one – but of course I mention this, not as laying stress upon it, but as an instance of God's mercy to me; – not that I can describe the feeling in words. – Then again I was much relieved next day, by being able to discover, (as I thought) sins in my conduct, which led God thus to fight against me. This He had been doing ever since I left Rome, and I from time to time had been impatient under the obstacles He put in my way, and had (as it were) asked why He did so. But now I came to think that there was some wilfulness in my coming to Sicily, as I did – and, tho' no one had advised me against it, yet I fancied I ought to have discovered they thought it an over-venturous thing. And then I felt more than I had done the wilfulness of my character generally – and I reflected that I was lying there the very day on which three years before I had sent in my resignation of the Tutorship (or something like it) – and, tho' I could not (and do not) at all repent the doing so, yet I began to understand that the *manner* was hasty and impatient. And then I recollected that the very day before I left Oxford, I had preached a University Sermon against wilfulness, so that I seemed to have been predicting my own condemnation. And I went on to ask myself whether I had not cherished resentment against the Provost – and whether in me was not fulfilled the text 1 Cor. XI. 29–32, (as I still think it has been). – But after all I was comforted by the thought that, in bringing myself into my present situation, I had not (as I just said) run counter to any advice given me – and I said 'I have not sinned against light –' and repeated this often. And then I thought I would try to obey God's will as far as I could, and, with a dreamy confused notion, which the fever (I suppose) occasioned, thought that in setting off the fourth day from Leonforte, I was walking as long as I could in the way of God's commandments, and putting myself in *the way* of His mercy, as if He would meet me, and surely so He did, as I lay in the hut – and though I have no distinct remembrance of the whole matter, yet it certainly seems like some instinct which He put within me and made me follow, to get me to Castro Giovanni, where I had a comfortable room, and was attended most hospitably and kindly. – It is most strange, and shows what is the hardness and inconsistency of my mind, that since I have been in England I have had hardly one feeling of joy and gratitude, tho' the thought of home drew tears into my eyes abroad, as oft as I thought of it – especially in my dreary voyage from Palermo to Marseilles.


# The Oxford Movement

*Extracts from a letter to John Bowden, a close friend of Newman from undergraduate days, and a lay-supporter of the Oxford Movement.*

August 31, 1833

Most probably I shall be in London the second week in October. It would give me real pleasure to find myself with you; and these are times when one's feelings and principles are tried so at every turn, that it is particularly needful to see one's friends often, to be sure how one is going on.

As to the state of the Church, I suppose it was in a far worse condition in Arian times, except in the one point you mention – that there was the *possibility* of true-minded men becoming bishops, which is now almost out of the question. If we had *one* Athanasius or Basil, we could bear with twenty Eusebius's, though Eusebius was not at all the worst of the bad. The scandals of Arian times are far worse than any now. I wish the Archbishop had somewhat of the boldness of the old Catholic prelates; no one can doubt he is a man of the highest principle, and would willingly die a martyr, but if he had but the little finger of Athanasius, he would do us all the good in the world. Things have come to a pretty pass when one must not speak as a Christian minister, for fear of pulling down the house over our heads. At the same time, I daresay, were I in high station, I should suddenly get very cautious from the feeling of responsibility. Well, it is a lucky thing to be able to talk; and I think we who can should make the most of it.

Under this feeling, we are just setting up here Societies for the Defence of the Church. We do not like our names known, but we hope the plan will succeed. We have already got assistants in five or six counties. Our objects are 'to rouse the clergy, to inculcate the Apostolical Succession, and to defend the Liturgy.' We hope to publish tracts, etc.

But one gains nothing by sitting still. I am sure the Apostles did not sit still: and agitation is the order of the day. I do not at all fear for the result, were we thrown on the people, though for a while many of us would be distressed *in re pecuniaria* – not that I would advocate a separation of Church and State unless the nation does more tyrannical things against us; but I do feel I should be glad if it were done and over, much as the nation would lose by it; for I fear the Church is being corrupted by the union.

*

*Extract from a letter to William Palmer, a member of the Oxford Movement.*

October 24, 1833

I would advocate a less formal scheme: not that I am not eventually for an Association, but not till the Bishop puts himself at our head in this or that diocese. I would merely exert myself in my own place, and with my own immediate friends, in declaring and teaching the half-forgotten truths of Church union and order to all within my influence. I address friends in other dioceses in turn, and urge them to do the same – in Keble's words, wishing them and our-selves to say to each other, 'We pledge ourselves to each other, reserving our canonical obedience'. We merely encourage and instruct each other: and, being able to say that others are doing elsewhere the same as we are, we have an excuse for being more bold: the circumstance that we have pledged ourselves allows us to introduce ourselves to strangers, etc. etc. We print and circulate tracts; our friends in other dioceses read them, approve, and partly disapprove. We say, 'Make what use you will of them, and alter them in your own way: reprint them and circulate them in turn, and send us yours to do the same with'. We try to get a footing in our county newspapers; and recommend our friends elsewhere to do the same. Thus gradually certain centres, in correspondence with each other and of a proselytising nature in their respective neighbourhoods, are formed.

You will see I am for no committee, secretaries, etc., but merely for certain individuals in every part of the country in correspondence with each other, instructing and encouraging each other, and acting with all their might in their respective circles.

*

*Extract from a letter to his former pupil, Robert Wilson, who became Keble's curate.*

March 31, 1834

The Church is certainly in a wretched state, but not a gloomy one to those who regard every symptom of dissolution as a ground of hope. Not that I would do any thing towards the undoing, or will fail both tooth and nail (so be it) to resist every change and degradation to which it is subjected. But, after all, I see a system *behind* the existing one, a system indeed which will take time and suffering to bring us to adopt, but still a firm foundation. Those who live by the breath of state patronage, who think the clergy must be gentlemen, and the Church must rest on the great, not the multitude, of course, are desponding. Woe to the profane hands who rob us of privilege or possession, but they can do us no harm. In the meantime, should (by any strange accident) the course of events fall back into its old channel, *I* will not be a disturber of the Church, though it is difficult to see how this return can be.

# Towards Rome

*Extract from a letter to his sister, Jemima.*

February 25, 1840

But this is not all. I begin to have serious apprehensions lest any religious body is strong enough to withstand the league of evil but the Roman Church. At the end of the first millenary it withstood the fury of Satan, and now the end of the second is drawing on.

Certainly the way that good principles have shot up is wonderful; but I am not clear that they are not tending to Rome – not from any necessity in the principles themselves, but from the much greater proximity between Rome and us than between infidelity and us, and that in a time of trouble we naturally look about for allies. I cannot say enough of the wonderful way in which the waters are rising here, and one should be very thankful. All this is a miserable prose, and regular talk worth nothing, and soon to be falsified by the event.

*

*Extract from a letter to Miss Giberne, a family friend who later became a Catholic nun, describing his plans for life at Littlemore.*

April 13, 1842

The truth is, I am just going to my new abode at Littlemore, and wish to get things into order. The papers give an absurdly exaggerated account of it, as you may suppose. I have long wished to live at Littlemore, and the difficulty has been to get a room for a library. Last Spring the heirs of old Costar turned a granary into a number of cottages, and I offered to rent them, on condition of their turning a stable which adjoined into a room (for books). This is the long and the short of the whole matter. I have taken my books there, and shall care little whether I get other inmates besides myself or not. Perhaps my curate will come – perhaps my school-master – perhaps my Secretary – perhaps some village boy who can be made something of – perhaps one or two pupils – perhaps some Oxford friends – some may stop for a permanence, some for a time. I shall attempt *very* little of a rule at first – though of course I am telling you all this as a secret – Perhaps, engaging every one to get up always at 6 o'clock – not to speak to each other except within certain hours – and perhaps to have but one sit-down meal in the day; – perhaps to pass certain hours in joint-devotion. I shall aim ultimately at dispensing with all servants. But it is all a dream at present. I shall do what I *can*, and I cannot say what I *shall* do, because I do not know what I can.

*

*Letter marked 'confidential' to Rev. James Mozley, explaining his decision to resign from the living of St Mary's Church, Oxford.*

September 1, 1843

Thank you for your most kind letter. I thought you would know already the prospect of my leaving St Mary's without my speaking to you of a subject which was *but* in prospect, and which (as you may think) makes me very sick. I have been thinking of it these three, I may say four, years, nor do I act without advice.

Really it is no personal feeling or annoyance under which I do it. I hope I am right in speaking openly to you, which I have not done but to a very few, but now I will tell you the real cause – which others besides those to whom I have said it may guess – but which (as far as I recollect) I have only told to Rogers, H. Wilberforce, R. Wilberforce, and Keble .... Tom may suspect it and Copeland, so may Church and Marriott. Indeed, I cannot name the limit of surmisers.

The truth then is, I am not a good son enough of the

Church of England to feel I can in conscience hold preferment under her. I love the Church of Rome too well.

Now please *burn this*, there's a good fellow, for you sometimes let letters lie on your mantelpiece.

\*

*Extract from a letter to his sister, Jemima, describing his emotions towards the Church of Rome.*

September 22, 1843

You cannot estimate what so many (alas!) feel at present, the strange effect produced on the mind when the conviction flashes, or rather pours, in upon it that Rome is the true Church. Of course it is a most revolutionary, and therefore a most exciting, tumultuous conviction. For this reason persons should not act under it, for it is impossible in such a state of emotion that they can tell whether their conviction is well founded or not. They cannot judge calmly.

It pains me very deeply to pain you, but you see how I am forced to it. You will not say, I think, that I am less affectionate to you from the bottom of my heart and loving, than I ever have been.

\*

*Letter to the sculptor, Richard Westmacott, describing his reasons for joining the Roman Catholic Church.*

July 11, 1845

It was very kind in you at the present time going into my matters. I suppose I may now tell you, that it is morally certain I shall join the R.C. Church, though I don't wish this *told* from me. It has been the conviction of six years – from which I have never receded. It was gained while outward circumstances were promising all around us, and every thing spoke of hope. I told my feeling to one or two persons who were about me in the autumn of 1839. I have waited patiently a long time.

My conviction has nothing whatever to do with events of the day. It is founded on my study of early Church history. I think the Church of Rome in every respect the continuation of the early Church. I think she is the early Church *in* these times, and the early Church is she *in* these times. They differ in doctrine and discipline as child and grown man differ, not otherwise. I do not see any medium between disowning Christianity, and taking the Church of Rome.

This being the ground of my conviction, I have at various times been reluctant to tell it to you – and I dare say seemed to you either reserved or afraid to argue. It was the latter – I was afraid. I will be frank with you, and tell you why. It was because I had got a notion that you had been inclined to scepticism – and it seemed a most serious thing to tell a person so inclined that one's own conviction was that he must believe everything or nothing. You have been so kindly persevering, from the interest you take in me, that I am forced to tell you my ground of conviction; and besides, I think you are stronger now than to be put out by such an avowal on my part. But for myself I say fairly, that I cannot believe only just as much as our Reformers out of their own heads have chosen we should believe – I must believe less or more. If Christianity is one and the same at all times, then I must believe, not what the Reformers have carved out of it, but what the Catholic Church holds.

I do not agree with Ward and Oakeley in their ground, but think you are hard on them. You call them disingenuous in trying to *stretch* the articles of our Church. Well then, do you wish them to *leave* our Church? that I suppose would not please you better. You abuse them for staying – you remonstrate with me for going. What middle course is there? I suppose, going into 'lay communion', giving up preferment, etc. and remaining quiet. This might be very well for a middle-aged, indolent person like myself – but do you really mean that a number of active, able men between 23 and 40, can think it their duty to waste their prime in doing nothing? Is it not a more fantastic idea than turning Mormonite or Jumper?

I am amused at your calling me 'cloistered –' it is true – but I am a sharper fellow than you think.

*

*Letter to John Keble written immediately after Newman's reception into the Church of Rome.*

November 14, 1845

May the Holy Trinity,
Father, Son, and Spirit,
return to you sevenfold, My dear Keble, all the good, of which you have been the instrument towards me, since I first knew you. To you I owe it, humanly speaking, that I am what and where I am. Others have helped me in various ways, but no one can I name but you, among those I ever knew, except one who is gone, who has had any part in setting my face in that special direction which has led me to my present inestimable gain.

Do not let me pain you, My dear Keble, by saying this. Let me not seem rude. Let it be your comfort, when you are troubled, to think that there is one who feels that he owes all to you, and who, though, alas, now cut off from you, is a faithful assiduous friend unseen.


## Early Catholic Days

*Letter to Elizabeth Bowden, who became a Catholic soon after Newman, concerning his plans for an Oratory in Birmingham.*

February 21, 1847

My first business this morning is to write to you – and you will be glad to be told, that, not only the day leads

33

me to do so, but that, as it happens, this very evening Mgr Brunelli (the Secretary of Propaganda) is to go to the Pope to gain his approbation to what I suppose is to be henceforth our calling. So many things succeed, one the other, in a place like this, that all this cannot but be abrupt to you – and I cannot in a few words explain all about it. I suppose we shall be *Oratorians*, that is, of the Congregation of St Philip Neri – we shall try to pass some time as Novices here in Italy; and if we can, we shall bring back a Father with us. Certain it is, we shall do our best to import a tradition, not to set up something for ourselves, which to me is very unpleasant. I still hope to be back at the time originally proposed – Dr Wiseman is very anxious for it – but I must leave all this in the hands of others. I shall keep this letter to tell you of Mgr's interview with the Pope. He proposes to get a Brief from him with such alterations of the Rule as will be necessary for England. I do not doubt we shall be backed up with all the Holy See can possibly do for us – and that (what is most anxious to say) all will depend on ourselves. In the Rule of St Philip this is especially the case – for as there are no vows, there is nothing to fall back on, but the personal religiousness and mutual love of the members, for the wellbeing of the body. I wish (but perhaps it is not right to wish) I had more confidence in myself – but I seem to have none. I cannot realise to myself that my time is not past – I may be of use by past recollections of me and by personal influence, to bring and keep others together – but that I shall be able to *do* any thing by myself, beyond being this bond of union, I do not feel. Indeed I do need the prayers of all friends, and you must all of you bear me in mind.

You will be disappointed, I fear, to be told what our duty will be – it will be to plant ourselves in a large town, say Birmingham, and attempt to get hold of those classes which at present are anything or nothing, members of clubs, mechanics-institutes, etc., etc. Not that this is not a great object, but perhaps you would not wish it for me. But it has great recommendations for me personally – It gives me what I want, active work, yet as much or as little as I wish – time for reading and writing – and a rule without being a very severe one. It will associate also together persons of very different tastes – as we want to argue, to preach, to sing and play, and to train young people. I trust we are doing what is intended for us. I have so many letters to write, that I shall make this a short one. Our mind has been made up ourselves sometime, but we have waited for letters from England. They came last Tuesday – since then, Mgr B. has wished to push the matter on. Love to the children.

*

*Extracts from his journal describing his personal difficulties in being a Catholic.*

April 8–17, 1847

I have in my mind a wound or cancer, the presence of which prevents me from being a good Oratorian. It cannot be described in a few words, for it is many-sided.

I am in the state of being able to fulfil my duty conscientiously along a prescribed course, but I cannot rise above it to a higher level. I creep along the ground, or even run – well enough for one who creeps or runs, but I cannot fly. I have not in me the elements required for rising or advancing.

So far as I know I do not desire anything of this world; I do not desire riches, power or fame; but on the other hand I do not like poverty, troubles, restrictions, inconveniences. Bad health I fear as one does who has experienced it, and avoid bodily pain more than I used to. I love the mean that lies between riches and poverty, and that is a temptation for me; yet I hope that without great difficulty I should be able to give up all that I have, if God ordered it.

I do not like a rule of life, although for eighteen years I have wished to live a more or less regular life. I like tranquillity, security, a life among friends, and among books, untroubled by business cares – the life of an Epicurean in fact. This state of mind, never strange to me, has grown with the years.

Although I have the fixed habit of referring all things to the will of God, and desire to do His will, and although in practice I really observe this principle in greater matters, yet I do not in practice seek His will in lesser things. And even in those greater matters, although I have often prayed earnestly to do His will, yet my actions have proceeded rather from a kind of conscientiousness which forbade me to act otherwise, from a sense of correctness, from perceiving what became me, and in doing which I should be consistent, than from faith and charity.

What is more serious, I have for some years fallen into a kind of despair and a gloomy state of mind. Not that I cannot say interiorly and with my whole heart; 'My God and my All', for these words have been constantly on my lips, but I have had many things to oppress me. In a variety of ways I have fallen away from hope. In the Church of England I had many detractors; a mass of calumny was hurled at me; my services towards that Church were misrepresented by almost everyone in authority in it. I became an exile in a solitude, where I spent some years with certain of my friends, but not even in that retreat was I safe from those who pursued me with their curiosity. I believe and hope that I did not on that account give way to anger, indignation, or the like, for in that respect I am not especially sensitive, but I was oppressed and lost hope. And now the cheerfulness I used to have has almost vanished. And I feel acutely that I am no longer young, but that my best years are spent, and I am sad at the thought of the years that have gone by; and I see myself to be fit for nothing, a useless log.

Then on becoming a Catholic I lost not a few of my friends, and that at a time when by death I had lost others most dear to me.

Further – when I lived in my retreat with certain others, seeking a way of life, we were accustomed to observe many things which are proper to Catholics – fasts, meditations, retreats, the use of the Breviary, and other practices belonging to the ecclesiastical, or rather to the religious life. And now I undergo a reaction, as they say, and have not the courage to continue those things which I did willingly in the Anglican Church.

But further still – it is difficult to explain and strange even to myself, but I have this peculiarity, that in the movement of my affections, whether sacred or human, my physical strength cannot go beyond certain limits. I am always languid in the contemplation of divine things, like a man walking with his feet bound together. I am held as it were by a fetter, by a sort of physical law, so that I cannot be forcible in preaching and speaking, nor fervent in praying and meditating.

\*

*Letter to Mary Holmes to whom Newman was spiritual director.*

July 31, 1850

I have been from home which will account for my silence. Else I should certainly have answered you sooner.

Never be afraid, my dear child, of telling any weakness to me, because we all have our faults, and those who take confessions of course hear many.

Do not be disheartened by these inconsistencies, whatever they may be, for your dear Lord will give you grace to overcome them.

As time goes on you will know yourself better and better. Time does that for us, not only by the increase of experience, but by the withdrawal of those natural assistances to devotion and self-surrender which youth furnishes. When the spirits are high and the mind fervent, though we may have waywardnesses and perverseness which we have not afterwards, yet we have something to battle against them. But when men get old, as I do, then they see how little grace is in them, and how much what seemed grace was but nature. Then the soul is left to lassitude, torpor, dejection, and coldness which is its real state, with no natural impulses, affections or imaginations to rouse it, and things which in youth seemed easy then become difficult. Then it finds how little self-command it has, and how little it can throw off the tempter when he comes behind and places it in a certain direction or position, or throws it down, or places his foot upon it. Then it understands at length its own nothingness, and that it has less grace than it had but it has nothing but grace to aid it. It is the sign of a saint to *grow*; common minds, even though they are in the grace of God, dwindle, (i.e. seem to do so) as times goes on. The energy of grace alone can make a soul strong in age.

Do not then be cast down, if you, though not *very* aged, feel less fervent than you did ten years since – only let it be a call on you to seek, grace to supply nature, as well as to overcome it. Put yourself ever fully and utterly into Mary's hands, and she will nurse you and bring you forward. She will watch over you as a mother over a sick child.

*

*Letter to George Ryder to whom Newman also gave spiritual direction.*

December 2, 1850

I am very glad to find you think you can keep your boys with you this winter. You can't do better, they will get good from being with you, and you will have companions. Give them my love.

I would not have you go to any mortifications. I will tell you what is the greatest – viz to do well the ordinary duties of the day. Determine to rise at a certain hour – to go through certain devotions – to give certain hours to your boys – Don't oppress yourself with them, but keep to your rules – and you will find it a sufficient trial.

Our Blessed Lady be with you whose great feast is coming, and all Saints and Angels.

*

*Letter to F W Faber, a former Anglican priest who followed Newman into the Roman Catholic Church and the Oratory, and became Father of a new Oratory in London; Newman came persistently into conflict with him over the running of the two houses and the relationship between them.*

December 30, 1851

I am going to write you a very ungracious letter, that is, to express my *sorrow* at your return.

The truth is, I have been fuming ever since you went, at the way you have been going on. I wrote to Malta to protest against your preaching – the letter missed you, and next I heard of you as lecturing an *Orat. Parv.* in Italian. The tone of your letter from Palermo pleased me not at all – I had no confidence in your sudden restoration, and I thought your letter excited. Then suddenly you were making for Rome, which was *forbidden* you – and before a letter could hit you, you are, against all medical orders, in England.

St Philip used to obey his physician. Have you taken one of the few opportunities a Father Superior has for obedience? I saw his letter – he prescribed six months for you.

You are *not* recovered – the very impatience with which you have come back shows it. As far as I can see, you are still bound to obey your medical adviser, and *explere numerum*. Your life is precious.

This, I know, is very ungracious but I am bound to say it.

## Latter Years

*Letter to Austin Mills, a fellow Oratorian, written during Newman's time as Rector of the Catholic University in Ireland.*

June 3, 1852

I fear this won't get to you in time. It struck me that, tho' I only spoke to the Bishop about the tonsure for our two novices, he might mean minor orders. If so, they must go up Friday night to Oscott. But it is useless writing now, when I have missed the post.

Tell Fr Nicholas I have made a great mistake about the size of my room. It is not more than 30 feet long at most – but it is certainly 17 or 18 feet high – and a fair width. It is, bating the wind which may come in at the window, the warmest room I could desire. The size precludes draughts, and the doors are all double with an interval between them.

When I got here, I found that the housekeeper, who would not let any other of the servants do it, had arranged, not only my clothes, but all my papers for me. I had put my letters in various compartments according to my relations towards them – and my Discourse papers, according as I had done with them or not. She had mixed everything, laying them most neatly according to their *size*. To this moment I have not had courage to attempt to set them right – and one bit, which was to have come in, I have from despair not even looked for. And so of my linen; I had put the linen in wear separate from the linen in reserve. All was revolutionised. I could find nothing of any kind. Pencils, pens, pen knife, tooth brush, boots, 'twas a new world – the only thing left, I suppose from a certain awe, was, (woe's me) my discipline.

Mind, everything was closed up, as far as they could be without lock and key, which I had not. She then came in to make an apology, but was so much amused at her own mischief, as to show she had no deep sense of its enormity.

I have found all sorts of useful books in the Bookcase – two copies of Shakespeare, Mitford's Greece, Aristotle's Ethics, Crabbe, Scott, Dryden, Wordsworth, Swift, Berkeley, Waverley Novels, Blackstone, Blair, Ovid and Gibbon.

*

*Extracts from his journal contrasting his previous life as a Protestant with his present one as a Catholic.*

January 21, 1863

O how forlorn and dreary has been my course since I have been a Catholic! here has been the contrast – as a Protestant, I felt my religion dreary, but not my life – but, as a Catholic, my life dreary, not my religion. Of course one's earlier years are (humanly speaking) best – and again, events are softened by distance – and I look back on my years at Oxford and Littlemore with tenderness – and it was the time in which I had a remarkable mission – but how am I changed even in look! till the affair of No 90 and my going to Littlemore, I had my mouth half open, and commonly a smile on my face – and from that time onwards my mouth has been closed and contracted, and the muscles are so set now, that I cannot but look grave and forbidding . . . . It began when I set my face towards Rome; and, since I made the great sacrifice, to which God called me, He has rewarded me in ten thousand ways, O how many! but he has marked my course with almost unintermittent mortification. Few indeed successes has it been His blessed will to give me through life. I doubt whether I can point to any joyful event of this world besides my scholarship at Trinity and my fellowship at Oriel – but since I have been a

Catholic, I seem to myself to have had nothing but failure, personally.

*

*Extracts from his journal in which he describes his conflict of attitudes with many of the leading Catholics in England.*

January 21, 1863

Rogers the other day asked Ward, Why it was that Catholics understood me so little! i.e. I suppose, why they thought so little of me. And the Saturday Review, writing apropos of my letter to the Globe of last summer, said that I had disappointed friends and enemies, since I had been a Catholic, by doing nothing. The reason is conveyed in the remark of Marshall of Brighton to Fr Ambrose last week: 'Why, he has made no converts as Manning and Faber have.' Here is the real secret of my 'doing nothing'. The only thing of course, which is worth producing, is *fruit* – but with the Cardinal, immediate *show* is fruit, and conversions the *sole* fruit. At Propaganda, conversions, and nothing else, are the proof of doing *any* thing. Everywhere with Catholics, to make converts, is doing something; and not to make them, is 'doing nothing'. And further still, in the estimate of Propaganda, of the Cardinal, and of Catholics generally, they must be splendid conversions of great men, noblemen, learned men, not simply of the poor. It must be recollected that at Rome they have had visions of the whole of England coming over to the Church, and that their notion of the instrumentality of this conversion *en masse*, is the conversion of persons of rank. *'Il governo'* is all in all in their ideas. Such an idea is perhaps even conveyed in our Brief, which sends us to the upper classes. Manning then and others are great, who live in London, and by their position and influence convert Lords and Ladies. This is what was expected of me .... To me conversions

were not the first thing, but the edification of Catholics
... The consequence is, that, so far from being
thought engaged in any good work, I am simply
discouraged and regarded suspiciously by the governing
powers as doing an actual harm.

*

*Letter to Margaret Wilson after the First Vatican
Council had defined the Infallibility of the Pope.*

October 20, 1870

It is a very difficult matter so to answer your sad letter
as to be real use to you – and, unless I can so write,
what is the use of writing at all?

I think there are some Bishops and Priests, who act
as if they did not care at all whether souls were lost or
not – and only wish to save souls on their own
measure. If you directly asked your Confessor, whether
you were obliged to receive the Pope's Infallibility,
you acted imprudently – if he asked you, he was not
only imprudent but cruel.

The rule in confession is, that when Priests differ in
opinion, you may choose, which you will. If I were
you, I should go to a Priest, who would not make it a
point to bring up this question – though I fear there
are few such in London.

Such unhappy times the Church has known before;
nay far worse, for there have been two or three Popes
at once, and the holiest men took opposite sides. It was
so in the early Church too, when divisions lasted for
20 or 30 years. We are not in so bad a case.

For myself, I have at various times in print professed
to hold the Pope's Infallibility; your difficulty is not
mine – but still I deeply lament the violence which
has been used in this matter.

However, there is a deeper question behind. When
you became a Catholic, you ought to have understood
that the voice of the Church is the voice of God. The
Church defines nothing that was not given to the

Apostles in the beginning, but that sacred deposit cannot be fully brought forward and dispensed except in the course of ages. It is not any argument against the Pope's Infallibility, that it was not defined as a truth till the 19th century.

Don't set yourself against the doctrine. Very little was passed, much less than its advocates wished – they are disappointed. Nothing is defined as to *what acts* are *ex cathedra*, nor to what things infallibility extends. Some people think the decree lessens the Pope's *actual* power.

*

*Letter to Lord Blachford on plans for a portrait of Newman to be painted by Ouless.*

March 10, 1877

I want you and Church to answer me a question. I am pressed to sit for an oil painting. I dislike it extremely and wish to get off – but, being pressed, I have said I would go by the judgement of friends – of course I should not mention your names.

What makes me so averse to it is the very reason why I am pressed to it. On account of the vile thing put into the Exhibition several years ago.

The case was this. Mr Boyle, now of Kidderminster, brother to Patrick Boyle whom you may recollect at Oriel, pressed me years ago, in the name of Birmingham parties, to let me be taken. I resisted it for three years – till at last it seemed so ungracious in me, that, after various refusals, I consented. My alleged (and a true) reason for declining was that I had done nothing for Birmingham, and had no claim for such a distinction, my personal reason was that I had no wish at all to be put in a collection together with a set of liberal party men or town celebrities with whom I had nothing in common.

At last I consented and a painter was sent to me who came with a theory, intending it most kindly, which

44

he gave in his defence, when my friends here cried out quite in grief, at his performance. He then said he meant to represent me as lamenting my Oxford position, circle, etc. etc.

Well, I suppose his employers did not like it either, for he could not get paid for it. A few weeks ago it was in a pawnbroker's shop – and lately has been bought as a speculation 'to be shown in the principal towns'.

I am now pressed by Mr Powell (of the firm of Hardman and Company) a Catholic, to let Mr W Ouless A.R.A. paint me. He wants to do it for nothing and give us here, the picture which probably we shall neither like nor have room for. And here again I shall act ungraciously if I refuse – and I write to you, not necessarily to decide for me, but because I cannot refuse unless I am backed up, and must to my great disgust give in.

*

*Extract from a letter to the Jesuit, Robert Whitty, on Newman's reluctance to be a Cardinal, an honour he received a year later.*

March 24, 1878

Perhaps you have seen in the Papers a wild article about me in relation to the Holy Father. I have reason to believe it was not Roman news but composed in London; and that in consequence of the action of some very kind friends and well-wishers of mine, persons known or unknown to me. But I trust nothing will come of it, I am far from making light of dignities, but under the example and shadow of St Philip, I may be allowed to decline them. They are much to be prized, both when they open on a man opportunities and channels of serving God, and again when they are a means of sanctioning and rewarding his past attempts at service. Now I am too old to do any thing new, and wish only to have time to set my house in order before I go; so that honours would not be in my case any means of usefulness.

*

*Letter to an old Anglican friend, George Edwards.*

February 24, 1887

My difficulty in writing breaks my thoughts and my feelings, and I not only can't say what I wish to say, but also my wishes themselves fare as if a dish of cold water was thrown over them.

I felt your letter, as all your letters, to be very kind to me and I feel very grateful to you. I don't know why you have been so kind, and you have been so more and more.

I will not close our correspondence without testifying my simple love and adhesion to the Catholic Roman Church, not that I think you doubt this; and did I wish to give a reason for this full and absolute devotion, what should, what can, I say, but that those great and burning truths, which I learned when a boy from evangelical teaching, I have found impressed upon my heart with fresh and ever increasing force by the Holy Roman Church? That Church has added to the simple evangelism of my first teachers, but it has obscured, dilute enfeebled, nothing of it – on the contrary, I have found a power, a resource, a comfort, a consolation in our Lord's divinity and atonement, in His Real Presence, in communion in His Divine and Human Person, which all good Catholics indeed have, but which Evangelical Christians have but faintly. But I have not strength to say more.

Thank you for the beautiful edition of the New Testament. I have a great dislike to heavy books.

# IDEAS

# Faith and Belief

It is love makes faith, not faith love. We are saved by that heavenly flame within us, which, while it consumes what is seen, aspires to what is unseen. Love is the gentle, tranquil, satisfied acquiescence and adherence of the soul in the contemplation of God; not only a preference of God before all things, but a delight in Him because He is God, and because His commandments are good; not only violent emotion or transport, but as St Paul describes it, long-suffering, kind, modest, unassuming, innocent, simple, orderly, disinterested, meek, pure-hearted, sweet-tempered, patient, enduring. Faith without Charity is dry, harsh, and sapless; it has nothing sweet, engaging, winning, soothing; but it was Charity which brought Christ down. Charity is but another name for the Comforter. It is eternal Charity which is the bond of all things in heaven and earth; it is Charity wherein the Father and the Son are one in the unity of the Spirit; by which the Angels in heaven are one, by which all Saints are one with God, by which the Church is one upon earth.

*Parochial and Plain Sermons, Vol IV*

As love worships God within the shrine, faith discerns Him in the world; and as love is the life of God in the solitary soul, faith is the guardian of love in our intercourse with men; and, while faith ministers to love, love is that which imparts to faith its praise and excellence.

And thus it is that faith is to love as religion to holiness; for religion is the Divine Law as coming to us from without, as holiness is the acquiescence in the same Law as written within. Love then is meditative, tranquil, pure, gentle, abounding in all offices of goodness and truth; and faith is strenuous and energetic, formed for this world, combating it, training the mind towards love, fortifying it in obedience, and overcoming sense and reason by representations more urgent than their own.

*Parochial and Plain Sermons, Vol IV*

True faith is what may be called colourless, like air or water; it is but the medium through which the soul sees Christ; and the soul as little really rests upon it and contemplates it, as the eye can see the air. When, then, men are bent on holding it (as it were) in their hands, curiously inspecting, analysing, and so aiming at it, they are obliged to colour and thicken it, that it may be seen and touched. That is, they substitute for it something or other, a feeling, notion, sentiment, conviction, or act of reason, which they may hang over, and dote upon. They rather aim at experiences (as they are called) within them, than at Him that is without them.

*Lectures on Justification*

Faith is a process of the Reason, in which so much of the grounds of inference cannot be exhibited, so much lies in the character of the mind itself, in its general view of things, its estimate of the probable and the improbable, its impressions concerning God's will, and its anticipations derived from its own inbred wishes, that it will ever seem to the world irrational and despicable; – till, that is, the event confirms it. The act of mind, for instance, by which an unlearned person savingly believes the Gospel, on the word of his teacher, may be analogous to the exercise of sagacity in a great statesman or general, supernatural grace doing for the uncultivated reason what genius does for them.

*Oxford University Sermons*

Was the religion of Christ propagated by the vehemence of faith and love, or by a philosophical balance of arguments? Look back at the early Martyrs, my brethren, what were they? why, they were very commonly youths and maidens, soldiers and slaves; – a set of hot-headed young men, who would have lived to be wise, had they not been obstinately set on dying first; who tore down imperial manifestoes, broke the peace, challenged the judges to dispute, would not rest till they got into the same den with a lion, and who, if chased out of one city, began preaching in another! So said the blind world about those who saw the Unseen. Yes! it was the spiritual sight of God which made them what they were. No one is a Martyr for a conclusion, no one is a Martyr for an opinion; it is faith that makes Martyrs.

*Discourses to Mixed Congregations*

Beware lest your religion be one of sentiment merely, not of practice. Men may speak in a high imaginative way of the ancient Saints and the Holy Apostolic Church, without making the fervour or refinement of their devotion bear upon their conduct. Many a man likes to be religious in graceful language; he loves religious tales and hymns, yet is never the better Christian for all this.

*Parochial and Plain Sermons, Vol I*

Creeds and dogmas live in the one idea which they are designed to express, and which alone is substantive; and are necessary only because the human mind cannot reflect upon that idea, except piecemeal, cannot use it in its oneness and entireness, nor without resolving it into a series of aspects and relations. And in matter of fact these expressions are never equivalent to it; we are able, indeed, to define the creations of our own minds, for they are what we make them and nothing else; but it were as easy to create what is real as to define it; and thus the Catholic dogmas are, after all, but symbols of a Divine fact, which, far from being compassed by those very propositions, would not be exhausted, nor fathomed, by a thousand.

*Oxford University Sermons*

The whole tenor of Scripture from beginning to end is to this effect: the matter of revelation is not a mere collection of truths, not a philosophical view, not a religious sentiment or spirit, not a special morality – poured out upon mankind as a stream might pour itself into the sea, mixing with the world's thought, modifying, purifying, invigorating it; – but an authoritative teaching, which bears witness to itself and keeps itself together as one, in contrast to the assemblage of opinions on all sides of it, and speaks to all men, as being ever and everywhere one and the same, and claiming to be received intelligently, by all whom it addresses, as one doctrine, discipline, and devotion directly given from above.

*Grammar of Assent*

Destroy religion, make men give it up, if you can; but while it exists, it will profess an insight into the next world, it will profess important information about the next world, it will have points of faith, it will have dogmatism, it will have anathemas. Christianity, therefore, ever will be looked on, by the multitude, what it really is, as a rule of faith as well as of conduct. Men may be Presbyterians, or Baptists, or Lutherans, or Calvinists, or Wesleyans; but something or other they will be; a creed, a creed necessary to salvation, they will have; a creed either in Scripture or out of it.

*Discussions and Arguments*

According as objects are great, the mode of attaining them is extraordinary; and again, according as it is extraordinary, so is the merit of the action. Here, instead of going to Scripture, or to a religious standard, let me appeal to the world's judgment in the matter. Military fame, for instance, power, character for greatness of mind, distinction in experimental science, are all sought and attained by risks and adventures. Courage does not consist in calculation, but in fighting against chances. The statesman whose name endures, is he who ventures upon measures which seem perilous, and yet succeed, and can be only justified on looking back upon them. Firmness and greatness of soul are shown, when a ruler stands his ground on his instinctive perception of a truth which the many scoff at, and which seems failing. The religious enthusiast bows the hearts of men to a voluntary obedience, who has the keenness to see, and the boldness to appeal to, principles and feelings deep buried within them, which they know not themselves, which he himself but by glimpses and at times realises, and which he pursues from the intensity, not the steadiness of his view of them. And so in all things, great objects exact a venture, and a sacrifice is the condition of honour.

*Oxford University Sermons*

Faith is illuminative, not operative; it does not force obedience, though it increases responsibility; it heightens guilt, it does not prevent sin.

*Difficulties of Anglicans, Vol I*

The natural man holds divine truths merely as an opinion, and not as a point of faith; grace believes, reason does but opine; grace gives certainty, reason is never decided.

*Discourses to Mixed Congregations*

A believing spirit is in all cases a more blessed spirit than an unbelieving. The testimony of unbelievers declares it: they often say, 'I wish I *could* believe; I should be happier, if I could; but my *reason* is unconvinced.'.

*Discussions and Arguments*

Faith is the first element of *religion*, and love, of *holiness*; and as holiness and religion are distinct, yet united, so are love and faith. Holiness can exist

without religion; religion cannot exist without holiness
. . . Holiness is love of the Divine Law.

*Parochial and Plain Sermons, Vol IV*

The safeguard of Faith is a right state of heart. This it
is that gives it birth; it also disciplines it. This is what
protects it from bigotry, credulity, and fanaticism. It is
holiness, or dutifulness, or the new creation, or the
spiritual mind, however we word it, which is the
quickening and illuminating principle of true faith,
giving it eyes, hands, and feet.

*Oxford University Sermons*

## The Spiritual Life

Man, with his motives and works, his languages, his
propagation, his diffusion, is from Him. Agriculture,
medicine, and the arts of life, are His gifts. Society,
laws, government, He is their sanction. The pageant
of earthly royalty has the semblance and the benedic-
tion of the Eternal King. Peace and civilisation,
commerce and adventure, wars when just, conquest
when humane and necessary, have His co-operation,
and His blessing upon them. The course of events, the
revolution of empires, the rise and fall of states, the
periods and eras, the progresses and the retrogressions
of the world's history, not indeed the incidental sin,
over-abundant as it is, but the great outlines and the
results of human affairs, are from His disposition.
The elements and types and seminal principles and
constructive powers of the moral world, in ruins
though it be, are to be referred to Him. He 'enlighteneth
ever man that cometh into this world'. His are the
dictates of the moral sense, and the retributive
reproaches of conscience. To Him must be ascribed
the rich endowments of the intellect, the irradiation of
genius, the imagination of the poet, the sagacity of the
politician, the wisdom (as Scripture calls it) which

now rears and decorates the Temple, now manifests itself in proverb or in parable. The old saws of nations, the majestic precepts of philosophy, the luminous maxims of law, the oracles of individual wisdom, the traditionary rules of truth, justice, and religion, even though imbedded in the corruption, or alloyed with the pride, of the world, betoken His original agency, and His long-suffering presence. Even where there is habitual rebellion against Him, or profound far-spreading social depravity, still the undercurrent, or the heroic outburst, of natural virtue, as well as the yearnings of the heart after what it has not, and its presentiment of its true remedies, are to be ascribed to the Author of all good.

*Idea of a University*

All that is good, all that is true, all that is beautiful, all that is beneficent, be it great or small, be it perfect or fragmentary, natural as well as supernatural, moral as well as material, comes from Him.

*Idea of a University*

We are not our own, any more than what we possess is our own. We did not make ourselves; we cannot be supreme over ourselves. We cannot be our own masters. We are God's property by creation, by redemption, by regeneration.

*Parochial and Plain Sermons, Vol V*

Nothing is more difficult than to realise that every man has a distinct soul, that every one of all the millions who live or have lived, is as whole and independent a being in himself, as if there were no one else in the whole world but he. To explain what I mean: do you think that a commander of an army realises it, when he sends a body of men on some dangerous service? I am not speaking as if he were wrong in so sending them; I only ask in matter of fact, does he, think you, commonly understand that each of those poor men has a soul, a soul as dear to himself, as precious in its nature, as his own? Or does he not rather look on the body of men collectively, as one mass, as parts of a whole, as but the wheels or springs of some great machine, to which he assigns the individuality, not to each soul that goes to make it up? . . .

Survey some populous town: crowds are pouring through the streets; some on foot, some in carriages; while the shops are full, and the houses too, could we see into them. Every part of it is full of life. Hence we gain a general idea of splendour, magnificence, opulence, and energy. But what is the truth? why, that every being in that great concourse is his own centre, and all things about him are but shades, but a 'vain shadow', in which he 'walketh and disquieteth himself in vain'. He has his own hopes and fears, desires, judgments, and aims; he is everything to himself, and no one else is really anything. No one outside of him can really touch him, can touch his soul, his immortality; he must live with himself for ever. He has a depth within him unfathomable, an infinite abyss of existence; and the scene in which he bears part for the moment is but like a gleam of sunshine upon its surface.

Again: when we read history, we meet with accounts of great slaughters and massacres, great pestilences, famines, conflagrations, and so on; and here again we are accustomed in an especial way to regard collections of people as if individual units. We cannot understand that a multitude is a collection of immortal souls.

I say immortal souls: each of those multitudes, not only *had* while he was upon earth, but *has* a soul, which did in its own time but return to God who gave it, and not perish, and which now lives unto Him. All those millions upon millions of human beings who ever trod the earth and saw the sun successively, are at this very moment in existence all together.

*Parochial and Plain Sermons, Vol IV*

The soul of man is intended to be a well-ordered polity, in which there are many powers and faculties, and each has its due place; and for these to exceed their limits is sin; yet they cannot be kept within those limits except by being governed, and we are unequal to this task of governing ourselves except after long habit. While we are learning to govern ourselves, we are constantly exposed to the risk, or rather to the occurrence, of numberless failures. We have failutres by the way, though we triumph in the end; and thus, as I just now implied, the process of learning to obey God is, in one sense, a process of sinning, from the nature of the case. We have much to be forgiven; nay, we have the more to be forgiven the more we attempt. The higher our aims, the greater our risks.

*Parochial and Plain Sermons, Vol V*

Our duty lies in acts – acts of course of every kind, acts of the mind, as well as of the tongue, or of the hand; but anyhow, it lies mainly in acts; it does not directly lie in moods or feelings. He who aims at praying well, loving sincerely, disputing meekly, as the respective duties occur, is wise and religious; but he who aims vaguely and generally at being in a spiritual frame of mind, is entangled in a deceit of words, which gain a meaning only by being made mischievous.

*Parochial and Plain Sermons, Vol II*

The Christian has a deep, silent, hidden peace, which the world sees not – like some well in a retired and shady place, difficult of access. He is the greater part of his time by himself, and when he is in solitude, that is his real state. What he is when left to himself and to his God, that is his true life. He can bear himself; he can (as it were) joy in himself, for it is the grace of God within him, it is the presence of the Eternal Comforter, in which he joys. He can bear, he finds it pleasant, to be with himself at all times – 'never less alone than when alone.' He can lay his head on his pillow at night, and own in God's sight, with overflowing heart, that he wants nothing – that he 'is full and abounds' – that God has been all things to him, and that nothing is not his which God could give him. More thankfulness, more holiness, more of heaven he needs indeed, but the thought that he can have more is not a thought of trouble, but of joy. It does not interfere with his peace to know that he may grow nearer God. Such is the Christian's peace, when, with a single heart and the Cross in his eye, he addresses and commends himself to Him with whom the night is as clear as the day.

*Parochial and Plain Sermons, Vol V*

Let those who have had seasons of seriousness, lengthen them into a life; and let those who have made good resolves in Lent, remember them in Eastertide; and let those who have hitherto lived religiously, learn devotion; and let those who have lived in good conscience, learn to live by faith; and let those who have made a good profession, aim at consistency; and let those who take pleasure in religious worship, aim at inward sanctity; and let those who have knowledge, learn to love; and let those who meditate, forget not mortification.

*Sermons on Subjects of the Day*

Be quite sure that resolute, consistent obedience, though unattended with high transport and warm emotion, is far more acceptable to Him than all those passionate longings to live in His sight, which look more like religion to the uninstructed. At the very best these latter are but the graceful beginnings of obedience, graceful and becoming in children, but in grown spiritual men indecorous, as the sports of boyhood would seem in advanced years. Learn to live by faith, which is a calm, deliberate, rational principle, full of peace and comfort.

*Parochial and Plain Sermons, Vol I*

They alone are able truly to enjoy this world, who begin with the world unseen. They alone enjoy it, who have first abstained from it. They alone can truly feast, who have first fasted; they alone are able to use the world, who have learned not to abuse it; they alone inherit it, who take it as a shadow of the world to come, and who for that world to come relinquish it.

*Parochial and Plain Sermons, Vol VI*

Man is born to obey quite as much as to command. Remove the true objects, and you do not get rid of a natural propensity: he will make idols instead; remove heaven, and he will put up with earth, rather than honour nothing at all. The principle of respect is as much a part of us as the principle of religion.

*Essays Critical and Historical, Vol I*

Men talk in a general way of the goodness of God, His benevolence, compassion, and long-suffering; but they think of it as of a flood pouring itself out all through the world, as the light of the sun, not as the continually repeated action of an intelligent and living Mind, contemplating whom it visits and intending what it effects. Accordingly, when they come into trouble, they can but say, 'It is all for the best – God is good', and the like; and this does but fall as cold comfort upon them, and does not lessen their sorrow, because they have not accustomed their minds to feel that He is a merciful God, regarding them individually, and not a mere universal Providence acting by general laws . . ..

God beholds thee individually, whoever thou art. He 'calls thee by thy name'. He sees thee, and understands thee, as He made thee. He knows what is in thee, all thy own peculiar feelings and thoughts, thy dispositions and likings, thy strength and thy weakness. He views thee in thy day of rejoicing, and thy day of sorrow. He sympathises in thy hopes and thy temptations. He interests Himself in all thy anxieties and remembrances, all the risings and fallings of thy spirit. He has numbered the very hairs of thy head and the cubits of thy stature. He compasses thee round and bears thee in His arms; He takes thee up and sets thee down. He notes thy very countenance, whether smiling or in tears, whether healthful or sickly. He looks tenderly upon thy hands and thy feet; He hears thy voice, the beating of thy heart, and thy very breathing. Thou dost not love thyself better than He loves thee. Thou canst not shrink from pain more than He dislikes thy bearing it; and if He puts it on thee, it is as thou wilt put it on thyself, if thou art wise, for a greater good afterwards. Thou art not only His creature (though for the very sparrows He has a care, and pitied the 'much cattle' of Nineveh), thou art man redeemed and sanctified, His adopted son, favoured with a portion of that glory and blessedness which flows from Him everlastingly unto the Only-begotten. Thou art chosen to be His, even above they fellows who dwell in the East and South. Thou wast one of those for whom Christ offered up His last prayer, and sealed it with His precious blood. What a thought is this, a thought almost too great for our faith!

*Parochial and Plain Sermons, Vol III*


# The Church and the World

The Church aims at three special virtues as reconciling and uniting the soul of its Maker: – faith, purity, and charity; for two of which the world cares little or nothing. The world, on the other hand, puts in the foremost place, in some states of society, certain heroic qualities; in others certain virtues of a political or mercantile character. In ruder ages, it is personal courage, strength of purpose, magnanimity; in more civilised, honesty, fairness, honour, truth and benevolence: – virtues, all of which, of course, the teaching of the Church comprehends, all of which she expects in their degree in all her consistent children, and all of which she enacts in their fulness in her saints; but which, after all, most beautiful as they are, admit of being the fruit of nature as well as of grace; which do not necessarily imply grace at all: which do not reach so far as to sanctify, or unite the soul by any supernatural process to the source of supernatural perfection and supernatural blessedness. Again, as I have already said, the Church contemplates virtue and vice in their first elements, as conceived and existing in thought, desire, and will, and holds that the one or the other may be as complete and mature, without passing forth from the home of the secret heart, as if it had ranged forth in profession and in deed all over the earth. Thus at first sight she seems to ignore bodies politic, and society, and temporal interests: whereas the world, on the contrary, talks of religion as being a matter of such private concern, so personal, so sacred, that it has no opinion at all about it.

*Difficulties of Anglicans, Vol I*

It is the peculiarity of the warfare between the Church and the world, that the world seems ever gaining on the Church, yet the Church is really ever gaining on the world. Its enemies are ever triumphing over it as vanquished, and its members ever despairing; yet it abides. It abides, and it sees the ruin of its oppressors and enemies. 'O how suddenly do they consume, perish, and come to a fearful end!' Kingdoms rise and fall; nations expand and contract; dynasties begin and end; princes are born and die; confederacies are made and unmade, and parties, and companies, and crafts, and guilds, and establishments, and philosophies, and sects, and heresies. They have their day, but the Church is eternal; yet in their day they seem of much account.

*Sermons on Subjects of the Day*

A large community, such as the Church, necessarily moves slowly; and this will particularly be the case when it is subject to distinct temporal rulers, exposed to various political interests and prepossessions, and embarrassed by such impediments to communication (physical or moral, mountains and seas, languages and laws) as separation into nations involves. Added to this, the Church is composed of a vast number of ranks and offices, so that there is scarcely any of her acts that belongs to one individual will, or is elaborated by one intellect, or that is not rather the joint result of many co-operating agents, each in his own place, and at his appointed moment . . ..

How different is the bearing of the temporal power upon the spiritual! Its promptitude, decisiveness, keenness, and force are well represented in the military host which is its instrument. Punctual in its movements, precise in its operations, imposing in its equipments, with its spirits high and its step firm, with its haughty clarion and its black artillery, behold, the mighty world is gone forth to war, with what? with an unknown something, which it feels but cannot see? which flits around it, which flaps against its cheek, with the air, with the wind. It charges and it slashes, and it fires its volleys, and it bayonets, and it is mocked by a foe who dwells in another sphere, and is far beyond the force of its analysis, or the capacities of its calculus.

*Difficulties of Anglicans, Vol I*

Such being the extreme difference between the Church and the world, both as to the measure and the scale of moral good and evil, we may be prepared for those vast differences in matters of detail, which I hardly like to mention, lest they should be out of keeping with the gravity of the subject, as contemplated in its broad principle. For instance, the Church pronounces the momentary wish, if conscious and deliberate, that another should be struck down dead, or suffer any other grievous misfortune, as a blacker sin than a passionate, unpremeditated attempt on the life of the Sovereign.

*Difficulties of Anglicans, Vol I*

Polished, delicate-minded ladies, with little of temptation around them, and no self-denial to practise, in spite of their refinement and taste, if they be nothing more, are objects of less interest to her, than many a poor outcast who sins, repents, and is with difficulty kept just within the territory of grace. Again, excess in drinking is one of the world's most disgraceful offences; odious it ever is in the eyes of the Church, but if it does not proceed to the loss of reason, she thinks it a far less sin than one deliberate act of detraction, though the matter of it be truth.

*Difficulties of Anglicans, Vol I*

The Church aims, not at making a show, but at doing a work. She regards this world, and all that is in it, as a mere shadow, as dust and ashes, compared with the value of one single soul. She holds that, unless she can, in her own way, do good to souls, it is no use her doing anything; she holds that it were better for sun and moon to drop from heaven, for the earth to fail, and for all the many millions who are upon it to die of starvation in extremest agony, so far as temporal affliction goes, than that one soul, I will not say, should be lost, but should commit one single venial sin, should tell one wilful untruth, though it harmed no one, or steal one poor farthing without excuse. She considers the action of this world and the action of the soul simply incommensurate, viewed in their respective spheres; she would rather save the soul of one single wild bandit of Calabria, or whining beggar of Palermo, than draw a hundred lines of railroad through the length and breadth of Italy, or carry out a sanitary reform, in its fullest details, in every city of Sicily, except so far as these great national works tended to some spiritual good beyond them.

*Difficulties of Anglicans, Vol I*

Look into the matter more steadily; it is very pleasant to decorate your chapels, oratories, and studies now, but you cannot be doing this for ever. It is pleasant to adopt a habit or a vestment; to use your office book or your beads; but it is like feeding on flowers, unless you have that objective vision in your faith, and that satisfaction in your reason, of which devotional exercises and ecclesiastical regulations are the suitable expression. Such will not last, on the long run, as are not commanded and rewarded by divine authority; they cannot be made to rest on the influence of individuals. It is well to have rich architecture, curious works of art, and splendid vestments, when you have a present God; but oh! what a mockery, if you have not! If your externals surpass what is within, you are, so far, as hollow as your evangelical opponents who baptise, yet expect no grace; or, as the latitudinarian writer I have been reviewing, who would make Christ's kingdom not of this world, in order to do a little more than the world's work. Thus your Church becomes, not a home, but sepulchre; like those high cathedrals, once Catholic, which you do not know what to do with, which you shut up and make monuments of, sacred to the memory of what has passed away.

*Difficulties of Anglicans, Vol I*

## Pain and Suffering

When a man's spirits are high, he is pleased with every thing; and with himself especially. He can act with vigour and promptness, and he mistakes this mere constitutional energy for strength of faith. He is cheerful and contented; and he mistakes this for Christian peace. And, if happy in his family, he mistakes mere natural affection for Christian benevolence, and the confirmed temper of Christian love. In short, he is in a dream, from which nothing could have saved him except deep humility, and nothing will ordinarily rescue him except sharp affliction.

*Parochial and Plain Sermons, Vol I*

I would go so far as to say, not only that pain does not commonly improve us, but that without care it has a strong tendency to do our souls harm, viz., by making us selfish; an effect produced, even when it does us good in other ways. Weak health, for instance, instead of opening the heart, often makes a man supremely careful of his bodily ease and well-being. Men find an excuse in their infirmities for some extraordinary attention to their comforts; they consider they may fairly consult, on all occasions, their own convenience rather than that of another. They indulge their wayward wishes, allow themselves in indolence when they really might exert themselves, and think they may be fretful because they are weak.

*Parochial and Plain Sermons, Vol III*

It is difficult to say which will comfort the worse, hearts hard from suffering, or hard from having never suffered; cruel despair, which rejoices in misery, or cruel pride, which is impatient at the sight of it. The cruelty, indeed, of the despairing is the more hateful, for it is more after Satan's pattern, who feels the less for others, the more he suffers himself; yet the cruelty of the prosperous and wanton is like the excesses of the elements, or of brute animals, not designed, more at random, yet perhaps even more keen and trying to those who incur it.

*Parochial and Plain Sermons, Vol V*

Who does not see that to bear pain well is to meet it courageously, not to shrink or waver, but to pray for God's help, then to look at it steadfastly, to summon what nerve we have of mind and body, to receive its attack, and to bear up against it (while strength is given us) as against some visible enemy in close combat? Who will not acknowledge that, when sent to us, we must make its presence (as it were) our own voluntary act, by the cheerful and ready concurrence of our own will with the will of God? Nay, who is there but must own that with Christ's sufferings before us, pain and tribulation are, after all, not only the most blessed, but even the most congruous attendants upon those who are called to inherit the benefit of them?

*Parochial and Plain Sermons, Vol III*

## Monks and Saints

If the truth must be spoken, what are the humble monk, and the holy nun, and other regulars, as they are called, but Christians after the very pattern given us in Scripture? What have they done but this – perpetuate in the world the Christianity of the Bible?

*Sermons on Subjects of the Day*

Monachism was one and the same everywhere, because it was a reaction from that secular life, which has everywhere the same structure and the same characteristics. And, since that secular life contained in it many objects, many states, and many occupations, here was a special reason, as a matter of principle, why the reaction from it should bear the badge of unity, and should be in outward appearance one and the same everywhere. Moreover, since that same secular life was, when monachism arose, more than ordinarily marked by variety, perturbation and confusion, it seemed on that very account to justify emphatically a rising and revolt against itself, and a recurrence to some state which, unlike itself, was constant and unalterable . . .

Serious men not only had a call, but every inducement which love of life and freedom could supply, to escape from its presence and its sway.

Their one idea then, their one purpose, was to be quit of it; too long had it enthralled them. It was not a question of this or that vocation, of the better deed, of the higher state, but of life and death. In later times a variety of holy objects might present themselves for devotion to choose from, such as the care of the poor, or of the sick, or of the young, the redemption of captives, or the conversion of the barbarians; but early monachism was flight from the world, and nothing else . . .

[Yet] the monks were not . . . dreamy sentimentalists, to fall in love with melancholy winds and purling rills, and waterfalls and nodding groves; but their poetry was the poetry of hard work and hard fare, unselfish hearts and charitable hands. They could plough and reap, they could hedge and ditch, they could drain; they could lop, they could carpenter; they could thatch, they could make hurdles for their huts; they could make a road, they could divert or secure the streamlet's bed, they could bridge a torrent . . .. If their grounds are picturesque, if their views are rich, they made them so, and had, we presume, a right to enjoy the work of their own hands. They found a swamp, a moor, a thicket, a rock, and they made an Eden in the wilderness.

To the monk heaven was next door; he formed no plans, he had no cares; the ravens of his father Benedict were ever at his side. He 'went forth' in his youth 'to his work and to his labour' until the evening of life; if he lived a day longer, he did a day's work more; whether he lived many days or few, he laboured on to the end of them. He had no wish to see further in advance of his journey than where he was to make his next stage. He ploughed and sowed, he prayed, he meditated, he studied, he wrote, he taught, and then he died and went to heaven.

*Historical Sketches, Vol II*

We are not accustomed to give to living men the *title* of saints, since *we* cannot well know, while they are among us, who have lived up to their calling and who have not. But in process of time, after death, their excellence perhaps get abroad; and then they become a witness, a specimen of what the Gospel can do, and a sample and a pledge of all those other high creations of God, His saints in full number, who die and are never known.

There are many reasons why God's saints cannot be known all at once; – first, as I have said, their good deeds are done in secret. Next, good men are often slandered, ridiculed, ill-treated in their lifetime; they are mistaken by those, whom they offend by their holiness and strictness, and perhaps they are obliged to withstand sin in their day, and this raises about them a cloud of prejudice and dislike, which in time indeed, but not till after a time, goes off. Then again their intentions and aims are misunderstood; and some of their excellent deeds or noble traits of character are known to some men, others to others, not all to all. This is the case in their lifetime; but after their death, when envy and anger have died away, and men talk together about them, and compare what each knows, their good and holy deeds are added up; and while they evidence their fruitfulness, also clear up or vindicate their motives, and strike the mind of survivors with astonishment and fear; and the Church honours them, thanks God for them, and 'glorifies God in' them ... If I am asked to state plainly how such a one differs from an ordinary religious man, I say in this – that he sets before him as the one object of life, to please and obey God; that he ever aims to submit his will to God's will; that he earnestly follows after holiness; and that he is habitually striving to have a closer resemblance to Christ in all things. He exercises himself, not only in social duties, but in Christian graces; he is not only kind, but meek; not only generous, but humble; not only persevering, but patient; not only upright, but forgiving; not only bountiful, but self-denying; not only contented, but meditative and devotional. An ordinary man thinks it enough to do as he is done by; he will think it fair to resent insults, to repay injuries, to show a becoming pride, to insist on his rights, to be jealous of his honour, when in the wrong refuse to confess it, to seek to be rich, to desire to be well with the world, to fear what his neighbours will say.

*Parochial and Plain Sermons, Vol IV*

I want to hear a Saint converse; I am not content to look at him as a statue; his words are the index of his hidden life, as far as that life can be known to man, for 'out of the abundance of the heart the mouth speaketh'. This is why I exult in the folios of the Fathers. I am not obliged to read the whole of them, I read what I can and am content . . ..

A Saint's writings are to me his real 'Life'; and what is called his 'Life' is not the outline of an individual, but either of the *auto-saint* or of a myth. Perhaps I shall be asked what I mean by 'Life'. I mean a narrative which impresses the reader with the idea of moral unity, identity, growth, continuity, personality. When a Saint converses with me, I am conscious of the presence of one active principle of thought, one individual character, flowing on and into the various matters which he discusses, and the different trans-actions in which he mixes. It is what no memorials can reach, however skilfully elaborated, however free from effort or study, however conscientiously faithful, however guaranteed by the veracity of the writers . . ..

Commonly, what is called 'the Life', is little more than a collection of anecdotes brought together from a number of independent quarters; anecdotes striking, indeed, and edifying, but valuable in themselves rather than valuable as parts of a biography; valuable whoever was the subject of them, not valuable as illustrating a particular Saint. It would be difficult to mistake for each other a paragraph of St Ambrose, or of St Jerome, or of St Augustine; it would be very easy to mistake a chapter in the life of one holy missionary or nun for a chapter in the life of another.

*Historical Sketches, Vol II*

## Education

All I say is, call things by their right names, and do not confuse together ideas which are essentially different. A thorough knowledge of one science and a superficial acquaintance with many, are not the same thing; a smattering of a hundred things or a memory for detail, is not a philosophical or comprehensive view. Recreations are not education; accomplishments are not education. Do not say, the people must be educated, when, after all, you only mean, amused, refreshed, soothed, put into good spirits and good humour, or kept from vicious excesses.

*Idea of a University*

That only is true enlargement of mind which is the power of viewing many things at once as one whole, of referring them severally to their true place in the universal system, of understanding their respective values, and determining their mutual dependence. Thus is that form of Universal Knowledge, of which I have on a former occasion spoken, set up in the individual intellect, and constitutes its perfection. Possessed of this real illumination, the mind never views any part of the extended subject matter of

Knowledge without recollecting that it is but a part, or without the associations which spring from this recollection. It makes everything in some sort lead to everything else.

*Idea of a University*

We know, not by a direct and simple vision, not at a glance, but, as it were, by piecemeal and accumulation, by a mental process, by going round an object, by the comparison, the combination, the mutual correction, the continual adaptation of many partial notions, by the employment, concentration, and joint action of many faculties and exercises of mind. Such a union and concert of the intellectual powers, such an enlargement and development, such a comprehensiveness, is necessarily a matter of training. And again, such a training is a matter of rule; it is not mere application, however exemplary, which introduces the mind to truth, nor the reading many books, nor the getting up many subjects, nor the witnessing many experiments, nor the attending many lectures. All this is short of enough; a man may have done it all, yet be lingering in the vestibule of knowledge: – he may not realise what his mouth utters; he may not see with his mental eye what confronts him; he may have no grasp of things as they are; or at least he may have no power of discriminating between truth and falsehood, of sifting out the grains of truth from the mass, of arranging things according to their real value, and, if I may use the phrase, of building up ideas. Such a power is the result of a scientific formation of mind; it is an acquired faculty of judgment, of clear-sightedness, of sagacity, of wisdom, of philosophical reach of mind, and of intellectual self-possession and repose – qualities which do not come of mere acquirement. The bodily eye, the organ for apprehending material objects, is provided by nature; the eye of the mind, of

71

which the object is truth, is the work of discipline and habit.

*Idea of a University*

An academical system without the personal influence of teachers upon pupils, is an arctic winter; it will create an ice-bound, petrified, cast-iron University, and nothing else.

*Historical Sketches, Vol III*

No conclusion is trustworthy which has not been tried by enemy as well as friend; no traditions have a claim upon us which shrink from criticism, and dare not look a rival in the face.

*Present Position of Catholics in England*

If then a practical end must be assigned to a University course I say it is that of training good members of society. Its art is the art of social life, and its end is fitness for the world. It neither confines its views to particular professions on the one hand, nor creates heroes or inspires genius on the other . . .. It aims at raising the intellectual tone of society, at cultivating the public mind, at purifying the national taste, at supplying true principles to popular enthusiasm and fixed aims to popular aspiration, at giving enlargement and sobriety to the ideas of the age, at facilitating the exercise of political power, and refining the intercourse of private life. It is the education which gives a man a clear conscious view of his own opinions and judgments, a truth in developing them, an eloquence in expressing them, and a force in urging them. It teaches him to see things as they are, to go right to the point, to disentangle a skein of thought, to detect what is sophistical, and to discard what is irrelevant . . .. He has the repose of a mind which lives in itself, while it lives in the world, and which has resources for its happiness at home when it cannot go abroad.

*Idea of a University*

Nothing is more common than for men to think that because they are familiar with words, they understand the ideas they stand for. Educated persons despise this fault in illiterate men who use hard words as if they comprehended them. Yet they themselves, as well as others, fall into the same error in a more subtle form, when they think they understand terms used in morals and religion, because such are common words, and have been used by them all their lives.

*Parochial and Plain Sermons, Vol I*

Really know what you say you know: know what you know and what you do not know; get one thing well before you go on to a second; try to ascertain what your words mean; when you read a sentence, picture it before your mind as a whole, take in the truth or information contained in it, express it in your own words, and, if it be important, commit it to the faithful memory. Again, compare one idea with another; adjust truths and facts; form them into one whole, or notice the obstacles which occur in doing so. This is the way to make progress; this is the way to arrive at results; not to swallow knowledge, but (according to the figure sometimes used) to masticate and digest it.

*Idea of a University*

The less a man knows, the more conceited he is of his proficiency; and, the more barbarous is a nation, the more imposing and peremptory are its claims.

*Historical Sketches, Vol I*

Education is a high word; it is the preparation for knowledge, and it is the imparting of knowledge in proportion to that preparation. We require intellectual eyes to know withal, as bodily eyes for sight. We need both objects and organs intellectual; we cannot gain them without setting about it; we cannot gain them in our sleep, or by haphazard. The best telescope does not dispense with eyes; the printing press or the lecture room will assist us greatly, but we must be true to ourselves, we must be parties in the work. A University is, according to the usual designation, an Alma Mater, knowing her children one by one, not a foundry, or a mint, or a treadmill.

*Idea of a University*

## Religion and Science

Much is said in this day by men of science about the duty of honesty in what is called the pursuit of truth – by 'pursuing truth' being meant the pursuit of facts. It is just now reckoned a great moral virtue to be fearless and thorough in inquiry into facts; and, when science crosses and breaks the received path of Revelation, it is reckoned a serious imputation upon the ethical character of religious men, whenever they show hesitation to shift at a minute's warning their position, and to accept as truths shadowy views at variance with what they have ever been taught and have held. But the contract between the cases is plain. The love and pursuit of truth in the subject-matter of religion, if it be genuine, must always be accompanied by the fear of error, of error which may be sin. An inquirer in the province of religion is under a responsibility for his reasons and for their issue.

*Via Media, Vol I*

In morals, as in physics, the stream cannot rise higher than its source. Christianity releases men from earth, for it comes from heaven; but human morality creeps, struts, or frets upon the earth's level, without wings to rise. [Science] does not contemplate raising man above himself; it merely aims at disposing of his existing powers and tastes, as is most convenient, or is practicable under circumstances. If finds him, like the victims of the French Tyrant, doubled up in a cage in which he can neither lie, stand, sit, nor kneel, and its highest desire is to find an attitude in which his unrest may be least. Or it finds him like some musical instrument, of great power and compass, but imperfect; from its very structure some keys must ever be out of tune, and its object, when ambition is highest, is to throw the *fault* of its nature where least it will be observed. It leaves man where it found him – man, and not an angel – a sinner, not a saint.

*Discussions and Arguments*

I say, you must use human methods *in their place*, and there they are useful; but they are worse than useless out of their place. I have no fanatical wish to deny to any whatever subject of thought or method of reason a place altogether, if it chooses to claim it, in the cultivation of the mind . . . . If in education, we begin with nature before grace, with evidences before faith, with science before conscience, with poetry before practice, we shall be doing much the same as if we were to indulge the appetites and passions, and turn a deaf ear to the reason.

*Discussions and Arguments*

The truth is that the system of Nature is just as much connected with Religion, where minds are not religious, as a watch or a steam-carriage. The material world, indeed, is infinitely more wonderful than any human contrivance; but wonder is not religion, or we should be worshipping our railroads. What the physical creation presents to us in itself is a piece of machinery, and when men speak of a Divine Intelligence as its Author, this god of theirs is not the Living and True, unless the spring is the god of a watch, or steam the creator of the engine. Their idol, taken at advantage (though it is *not* an idol, for they do not worship it), is the animating principle of a vast and complicated system; it is subjected to laws, and it is connatural and coextensive with matter.

Take the system of Nature by itself, detached from the axioms of Religion, and I am willing to confess – nay, I have been expressly urging – that it does not force us to take it for *more* than a system; but why, then, persist in calling the study of it religious, when it can be treated, and is treated, thus atheistically? Say that Religion hallows the study, not that the study is a true ground of Religion. The essence of Religion is the idea of a Moral Governor, and a particular Providence; now let me ask, is the doctrine of moral governance and a particular providence conveyed to us through the physical sciences at all?

I consider, then, that intrinsically excellent and noble as are scientific pursuits, and worthy of a place in a liberal education, and fruitful in temporal benefits to the community, still they are not, and cannot be, *the instrument* of an ethical training; that physics do not supply a basis, but only materials for religious sentiment; that knowledge does but occupy, does not form the mind; that apprehension of the unseen is the only known principle capable of subduing moral evil, educating the multitude, and organising society; and that, whereas man is born for action, action flows not from inferences, but from impressions – not from reasonings, but from Faith.

*Discussions and Arguments*

There is no unrestrained, no lawless freedom in the physical world – after the pattern of its Maker. It is not, indeed, good as He is good, even in its own degree; for it is full of fault and imperfection, and might be better than it is. It is not wise as He is wise; rather it has no intelligence at all lodged in it. It is not stable as He is stable; but, on the contrary, it is ever in motion and ever on the change. But one attribute it has of God, without exception or defect, and that is the attribute of order.

*Sermons on Various Occasions*

Whenever we look abroad, we are reminded of those most gracious and holy Beings, the servants of the Holiest, who deign to minister to the heirs of salvation. Every breath of air and ray of light and heat, every beautiful prospect, is, as it were, the skirts of their garments, the waving of the robes of those whose faces see God in heaven.

*Parochial and Plain Sermons, Vol II*

How much has every herb and flower in it to surprise and overwhelm us! For, even did we know as much about them as the wisest of men, yet there are those around us, though unseen, to whom our greatest knowledge is as ignorance; and, when we converse on subjects of Nature scientifically, repeating the names of plants and earths, and describing their properties, we should do so religiously, as in the hearing of the great Servants of God.

*Parochial and Plain Sermons, Vol II*

A man who is religious, is religious morning, noon, and night; his religion is a certain character, a mould in which his thoughts, words, and actions are cast, all forming parts of one and the same whole. He sees God in all things; every course of action he directs towards those spiritual objects which God has revealed to him; every occurrence of the day, every event, every person met with, all news which he hears, he measures by the standard of God's will. And a person who does this may be said almost literally to pray without ceasing.

*Parochial and Plain Sermons, Vol VII*

# England and the English

The Englishman is indeed rough, surly, a bully and a bigot; these are his weak points: but if ever there was a generous, good, tender heart, it beats within his breast. Most placable, he forgives and forgets: forgets, not only the wrongs he has received, but the insults he has inflicted. Such he is commonly; for doubtless there are times and circumstances in his dealings with foreigners in which, whether when in despair or from pride, he becomes truculent and simply hateful; but at home his bark is worse than his bite. He has qualities, excellent for the purposes of neighbourhood and intercourse; – and he has, besides, a shrewd sense, and a sobriety of judgment, and a practical logic, which passion does not cloud, and which makes him understand that good-fellowship is not only commendable, but expedient too. And he has within him a spring of energy, pertinacity, and perseverance, which makes him as busy and effective in a colony as he is companionable at home. Some races do not move at all; others are ever jostling against each other; the Englishman is ever stirring, yet never treads too hard upon his fellow-countryman's toes. He does his work neatly, silently, in his own place; he looks to himself, and can take care of himself; and he has that instinctive veneration for the law, that he can worship it even in the abstract, and thus is fitted to go shares with others all around him in that political sovereignty, which other races are obliged to concentrate in one ruler.

*Discussions and Arguments*

If there is one passion more than another which advantageously distinguishes the Englishman, it is that of personal attachment. He lives in the present, in contrast to the absent and the past. He ignores foreigners at a distance! but when they come to him, if they come recommended by their antecedents, and make an appeal to his eyes and his ears, he almost worships them.

*Present Position of Catholics in England*

England, surely, is the paradise of little men, and the purgatory of great ones.

*Discussions and Arguments*

# POETRY

# My God and King

Let me always, my God and King
   In Thy dear Name rejoice
And daily to Thy praises sing
   With ever grateful voice.
I am a worm, and Thou art good
   To save a wretch like me,
Who always has Thy grace withstood,
   And turned his back on Thee.
O grant that I may persevere
   And finally obtain
A glorious crown, purchased for dear,
   That ever may remain.
Purchased for dear, for by the Blood
   Of Jesus it is given,
Who suffered death, the Just and Good,
   That we may live in heaven.
O may I scorn each mundane joy,
   And meditate on Thee.
May heaven all my thoughts employ,
   Then happy shall I be.

*1816: when Newman was aged fifteen, at the time of
his first conversion.*

# Solitude

There is in stillness oft a magic power
To calm the breast, when struggling passions lower;
Touch'd by its influence, in the soul arise
Diviner feelings, kindred with the skies.

By this the Arab's kindling thoughts expand
When circling skies enclose the desert sand;
For this the hermit seeks the thickest grove,
To catch th' inspiring glow of heavenly love.
It is not solely in the freedom given
To purify and fix the heart on heaven;
There is a Spirit singing aye in air,
That lifts us high above all mortal care.
No mortal measure swells that mystic sound,
No mortal minstrel breathes such tones around –
The Angels' hymn – the sovereign harmony
That guides the rolling orbs along the sky –
And hence perchance the tales of saints who view'd
And heard Angelic choirs in solitude,
By most unheard – because the earthly din
Of toil or mirth has charms their ears to win
Alas for man! he knows not of the bliss,
The heaven that brightens such a life as this.

*1818: while Newman was an undergraduate at Oxford.*

## The Sign of the Cross

Whene'er across this sinful flesh of mine
    I draw the Holy Sign,
All good thoughts stir within me and renew
    Their slumbering strength divine;
Till there springs up a courage high and true
    To suffer and to do.

And who shall say, but hateful spirits round,
    For their brief hour unbound.

Shudder to see, and wail their overthrow?
   While on far heathen ground
Some lonely Saint hails the fresh odour, though
   Its source he cannot know.

November 1832: Oxford.

## The Haven

Whence is this awe, by stillness spread
   O'er the world-fretted soul?
Wave reared on wave its godless head,
While my keen bark, by breezes sped,
Dash'd fiercely through the ocean bed,
   And chafed toward its goal.

But now there reigns so deep a rest,
   That I could almost weep.
Sinner! thou hast in this rare guest
Of Adam's peace a figure blest;
'Tis Eden seen, though not possess'd,
   Which cherub-flames still keep.

December 1832: in Gibraltar at the beginning of his<br>Mediterranean travels.

## Sensitiveness

Time was, I shrank from what was right
   From fear of what was wrong;
I would not brave the sacred fight,
   Because the foe was strong.

But now I cast that finer sense
   And sorer shame aside;

Such dread of sin was indolence,
   Such aim at Heaven was pride.

So, when my Saviour calls, I rise,
   And calmly do my best;
Leaving to Him, with silent eyes
   Of hope and fear, the rest.

I step, I mount where He has led –
   Men count my haltings o'er –
I know them yet, though self I dread,
   I love His precept more.

*January 1833; Malta*


## Heaven's Letters

When Heaven sends sorrow,
   Warnings go first,
   Lest it should burst
   With stunning might
   On souls too bright
To fear the morrow

Can science bear us
   To the hid springs
   Of human things?
   Why may not dream
   Or thought's day gleam
Startle, yet cheer us?

Are such thoughts fetters,
   While Faith disowns
   Dread of earth's tones,
   Recks but Heaven's call,
   And on the wall
Reads but Heaven's letters?

*February 1833: at sea.*

# The Pillar of the Cloud

Lead, Kindly Light, amid the encircling gloom,
    Lead Thou me on!
The night is dark, and I am far from home –
    Lead Thou me on!
Keep Thou my feet; I do not ask to see
The distant scene – one step enough for me.

I was not ever thus, nor pray'd that Thou
    Shouldst lead me on.
I loved to choose and see my path, but now
    Lead Thou me on!
I loved the garish day, and, spite of fears,
Pride ruled my will: remember not past years.

So long Thy power hath blest me, sure it still
    Will lead me on,
O'er moor and fen, o'er crag and torrent, till
    The night is gone;
And with the morn those angel faces smile
Which I have loved long since, and lost awhile.

*June 1833: at sea on his journey home after his illness*
*in Sicily.*

# The Elements

Man is permitted much
    To scan and learn
    In Nature's frame;
Till he well-nigh can tame
Brute mischiefs and can touch
    Invisible things, and turn
All warring ills to purposes of good.
    Thus, as a god below,

He can control,
And harmonise, what seems amiss to flow
　As sever'd from the whole
　And dimly understood.

But o'er the elements
　　One Hand alone
　　One Hand has sway.
What influence day by day
In straiter belt prevents
The impious Ocean, thrown
Alternate o'er the ever-sounding shore?
　　Or who has eye to trace
　　　How the Plague came?
Forerun the doublings of the Tempest's race?
　　Or the Air's weight and flame
　　On a set scale explore?

　　Thus God has will'd
　　That man, when fully skill'd,
　　Still gropes in twilight dim;
　　Encompass'd all his hours
　　　By fearfullest powers
　　　Inflexible to him.
　　That so he may discern
　　　His feebleness,
　　And e'en for earth's success
　　　To Him in wisdom turn,
Who holds for us the keys of either home,
Earth and the world to come.

*June 1833: at sea on his homeward journey.*


# Morning

I rise and raise my clasped hands to Thee!
Henceforth, the darkness hath no part in me,
　Thy sacrifice this day;

Abiding firm, and with a freeman's might
Stemming the waves of passion in the fight –
   Ah, should I from Thee stray,
My hoary head, Thy table where I bow,
Will be my shame, which are mine honour now.
Thus I set out – Lord! lead me on my way!

*1834: Oxford.*


# Evening

O Holiest Truth! how have I lied to Thee!
I vow'd this day Thy festival should be:
   But I am dim ere night.
Surely I made my prayer, and I did deem
That I could keep in me Thy morning beam,
   Immaculate and bright.
But my foot slipp'd; and, as I lay, he came,
My gloomy foe, and robb'd me of heaven's flame.
Help Thou my darkness, Lord, till I am light.

*1834: Oxford.*


# The Dream of Gerontius
*(Selections from a poetic drama of a soul
entering the after-life)*

Gerontius

Jesu, Maria – I am near to death,
   And Thou art calling me; I know it now.
Not by the token of this faltering breath,
   This chill at heart, this dampness on my brow, –

(Jesu, have mercy! Mary, pray for me!)
    'Tis this new feeling, never felt before,
(Be with me, Lord, in my extremity!)
    That I am going, that I am no more.
'Tis this strange innermost abandonment,
    (Lover of souls! great God! I look to Thee,)
This emptying out of each constituent
    And natural force, by which I come to be.
Pray for me, O my friends; a visitant
    Is knocking his dire summons at my door,
The like of whom, to scare me and to daunt,
    Has never, never come to me before;
'Tis death,–O loving friends, your prayers! – 'tis he!...
As though my very being had given way,
    As though I was no more a substance now,
And could fall back on nought to be my stay,
    (Help, loving Lord! Thou art my sole Refuge,
        Thou,)
And turn no whither, but must needs decay
    And drop from out the universal frame
Into that shapeless, scopeless, blank abyss,
    That utter nothingness, of which I came:

This is it that has come to pass in me;
Oh, horror! this it is, my dearest, this;
So pray for me, my friends, who have not strength to
       pray....


Rouse thee, my fainting soul, and play the man;
    And through such waning span
Of life and thought as still has to be trod,
    Prepare to meet thy God.
And while the storm of that bewilderment
    Is for a season spent,
And, ere afresh the ruin on me fall,
    Use well the interval....

Firmly I believe and truly
   God is Three, and God is One;
And I next acknowledge duly
   Manhood taken by the Son.
And I trust and hope most fully
   In that manhood crucified;
And each thought and deed unruly
   Do to death, as He has died.
Simply to His grace and wholly
   Light and life and strength belong,
And I love, supremely solely,
   Him the holy, Him the strong. . . .

I can no more; for now it comes again,
That sense of ruin, which is worse than pain,
That masterful negation and collapse
Of all that makes me man; as though I bent
Over the dizzy brink
Of some sheer infinite descent;
Or worse, as though
Down, down for ever I was falling through
The solid framework of created things,
And needs must sink and sink
Into the vast abyss. And, crueller still,
A fierce and restless fright begins to fill
The mansion of my soul. . . .

Novissima hora est; and I fain would sleep.
The pain has wearied me . . . Into Thy hands,
O Lord, into Thy hands . . .

Soul of Gerontius

I went to sleep; and now I am refresh'd,
A strange refreshment: for I feel in me
An inexpressive lightness, and a sense
Of freedom, as I were at length myself,

And ne'er had been before. How still it is!
I hear no more the busy beat of time,
No, nor my fluttering breath, nor struggling pulse;
Nor does one moment differ from the next.
I had a dream; yes: – some one softly said
'He's gone;' and then a sigh went round the room.
And then I surely heard a priestly voice
Cry 'Subvenite;' and they knelt in prayer.
I seem to hear him still; but thin and low,
And fainter and more faint the accents come,
As at an ever-widening interval.
Ah! whence is this? What is this severance?
This silence pours a solitariness
Into the very essence of my soul;
And the deep rest, so soothing and so sweet,
Hath something too of sternness and of pain.
For it drives back my thoughts upon their spring
By a strange introversion, and perforce
I now begin to feed upon myself,
Because I have nought else to feed upon.


Angel

My work is done,
   My task is o'er,
      And so I come,
         Taking it home,
For the crown is won,
      Alleluia,
   For evermore.

My Father gave
   In charge to me
      This child of earth
      E'en from its birth,
To serve and save,
      Alleluia,
   And saved is he.

This child of clay
  To me was given,
    To rear and train
    By sorrow and pain
In the narrow way,
    Alleluia.
  From earth to heaven.


Soul

Now know I surely that I am at length
Out of the body; had I part with earth,
I never could have drunk those accents in,
And not have worshipp'd as a god the voice
That was so musical; but now I am
So whole of heart, so calm, so self-possess'd,
With such a full content, and with a sense
So apprehensive and discriminant,
As no temptation can intoxicate.
Nor have I even terror at the thought
That I am clasp'd by such a saintliness.


First Choir of Angelicals

Praise to the Holiest in the height,
  And in the depth be praise:
In all His words most wonderful;
  Most sure in all His ways!

To us His elder race He gave
  To battle and to win,
Without the chastisement of pain,
  Without the soil of sin.

The younger son He will'd to be
  A marvel in his birth:

Spirit and flesh his parents were;
  His home was heaven and earth.

The Eternal bless'd His child, and arm'd,
  And sent him hence afar,
To serve as champion in the field
  Of elemental war.

To be His Viceroy in the world
  Of matter, and of sense;
Upon the frontier, towards the foe,
  A resolute defence.


Soul

The sound is like the rushing of the wind –
The summer wind – among the lofty pines;
Swelling and dying, echoing round about,
Now here, now distant, wild and beautiful;
While, scatter'd from the branches it has stirr'd,
Descend ecstatic odours.


Fifth Choir of Angelicals

Praise to the Holiest in the height,
  And in the depth be praise:
In all His words most wonderful;
  Most sure in all His ways!

O loving wisdom of our God!
  When all was sin and shame,
A second Adam to the fight
  And to the rescue came.

O wisest love! that flesh and blood
  Which did in Adam fail,

94

Should strive afresh against their foe,
　　Should strive and should prevail;

And that a higher gift than grace
　　Should flesh and blood refine,
God's Presence and His very Self,
　　And Essence all-divine.

O generous love! that He who smote
　　In man for man the foe,
The double agony in man
　　For man should undergo;

And in the garden secretly,
　　And on the cross on high,
Should teach His brethren and inspire
　　To suffer and to die.


Angel

　　. . . Praise to His Name!
The eager spirit has darted from my hold,
And, with intemperate energy of love,
Flies to the dear feet of Emmanuel;
But, ere it reach them, the keen sanctity,
Which with its effluence, like a glory, clothes
And circles round the Crucified, has seized,
And scorch'd, and shrivell'd it; and now it lies
Passive and still before the awful Throne.
O happy, suffering soul! for it is safe,
Consumed, yet quicken'd, by the glance of God.


Soul

Take me away, and in the lowest deep
　　There let me be,

And there in hope the lone night-watches keep,
  Told out for me.
There, motionless and happy in my pain,
  Lone, not forlorn, –
There will I sing my sad perpetual strain,
  Until the morn.
There will I sing, and soothe my stricken breast,
  Which ne'er can cease
To throb, and pine, and languish, till possest
  Of its Sole Peace.
There will I sing my absent Lord and Love: –
  Take me away;
That sooner I may rise, and go above
And see Him in the truth of everlasting day.


Angel

Softly and gently, dearly-ransom'd soul,
  In my most loving arms I now enfold thee,
And, o'er the penal waters, as they roll,
  I poise thee, and I lower thee, and hold thee.

And carefully I dip thee in the lake,
  And thou, without a sob or a resistance,
Dost through the flood thy rapid passage take,
  Sinking deep, deeper, into the dim distance.

Angels, to whom the willing task is given,
  Shall tend, and nurse, and lull thee, as thou liest;
And Masses on the earth, and prayers in heaven,
  Shall aid thee at the throne of the Most Highest.

Farewell, but not for ever, brother dear,
  Be brave and patient on thy bed of sorrow;
Swiftly shall pass thy night of trial here,
  And I will come and wake thee on the morrow.

*1865: The Oratory, Birmingham: written when
          Newman thought he was dying.*

96

# Bibliography

A good biography of Newman based on extensive research is *John Henry Newman* by C. S. Dessain (Oxford University Press, 1980).

*Newman*, by Owen Chadwick (Oxford University Press, 1983), offers profound reflections on his thoughts and ideas.

In *Letters and Correspondence of J. H. Newman*, (Longman Co., 1891), Anne Mozley has selected letters from Newman's Anglican years.

*A Packet of Letters*, edited by Joyce Sugg (Oxford University Press, 1983), is an excellent selection of letters from throughout Newman's life. It contains helpful short biographies of his correspondents.

*John Henry Newman Autobiographical Writings*, edited by Henry Tristram (Sheed & Ward, 1957), is a fascinating collection of extracts from his journals and letters.

*A Newman Treasury*, edited by C. F. Harrold (1943), is an American publication giving lengthy extracts from his prose works.

There is an Everyman edition of Newman's spiritual autobiography *Apologia Pro Vita Sua* (J. M. Dent & Sons, 1912).

Dimension Books have produced a small volume of Newman's poetry, simply titled *Hymns*.

*Other Lamp Press titles*

# HEARTS SET ON THE PILGRIMAGE

*Joan Puls OSF*

Joan Puls challenges congregations, communities and individual Christians to discover a common discipleship that will lead to a dramatic and thoroughgoing renewal of the Church.

In a series of reflections, she looks at the Church as servant, as offering hospitality, heralding good news, reconciling, prophesying, suffering and celebrating.

# THE LAMP SAINTS SERIES

# HILDA

*Anne Warin*

In the first volume of the new Lamp Saints series, Anne Warin tells the story of Hilda, foundress of the Monastery of Whitby in 657.

In a narrative that is part fact and part fiction Anne Warin welds together the dramatic events of Anglo Saxon time, the synod of Whitby, the personalities of the saints and the upsurge of scholarship and art. The life of Hilda provides many comparisons and contrasts with the life of women in today's Church.

# THE LAMP VISION OF . . . SERIES

# LAMENT AND LOVE: THE VISION OF GEORGE HERBERT

*Edited by Robert Van de Weyer*

The first book in the Lamp Vision of . . . series is an anthology of extracts from the work of the great seventeenth century poet and parson. The extracts are especially chosen to define his unique Christian vision.

# THE SPIRITUAL KISS: THE VISION OF SAINT AELRED OF RIEVAULX

*Edited by Robert Van de Weyer and Pat Saunders*

In this third volume in the Vision of . . . series, the life of Aelred, the official biographer of Edward the Confessor, is considered in the light of his writing. He was a writer in the mystical tradition, severe in his interpretation of the monastic rule but with a genius for friendship. The 'spiritual kiss' to which the title refers is given 'not by the touch of the mouth but by the affection of the heart'.

# HIDDEN HEROES OF THE GOSPELS
## Feminine Counterparts of Jesus

*Joseph A. Grassi*

In this fascinating new book, Joseph Grassi studies the Gospels as narrative drama, and discovers that the ideal disciple is often portrayed as a woman. Pursuing a detailed analysis of the literary structure of each of the four Gospels, Grassi shows how the text works to point out the model forms of discipleship, and how women fit this model. Among the women portrayed are the poor widow in the Temple, the daughter of Jairus, the Syro-Phoenician woman, and Mary Magdalene. £4.99

# A NON-VIOLENT LIFESTYLE
## Conversations with Jean and Hildegard Goss-Mayr

*Gérard Houver*

Jean and Hildegard Goss-Mayr have spent their lives spreading abroad their message of non-violence. Nominated for the Nobel Peace Prize, they have given seminars throughout the world. £4.99

# DRAW NEAR TO GOD
## Daily Meditations with Pope John Paul II

In daily meditations throughout the church year, the Pope reflects on the place of marriage, family and work in the Christian's life. He challenges all Christians to respect life, to evangelise and to bring the peace of Christ to a weary world. £4.99

# THE WARSAW GHETTO
## A Christian's Testimony

*Wladyslaw Bartoszewski*

Wladyslaw Bartoszewski, a Roman Catholic, offers here a rare testimony to the shared fate of Warsaw's inhabitants during the Holocaust of World War II. His unique and moving book tells the story of the Warsaw ghetto from the unusual perspective of one of the few ethnic Poles to have come to the aid of the Jews during the war. At great peril to his own life, he worked to save some of the Jews and to publicise the events taking place in Poland to an unbelieving world.